"Joseph Farah raises a clarion call to action in his new book, *Taking America Back*. He hits the nail on the head on every issue. What's more, he lays the blame for America's problems right where it belongs—in the lap of liberalism. His insightful analysis of what he calls 'this evil ideology' is worth the price of the book. Don't miss it!"

— **Dr. Jerry Falwell**
Founder and Chancellor,
Liberty University
Lynchburg, Virginia

"Taking America Back is a wakeup call for responsible self-government. It's a radical vision for liberty—in the same way Washington, Jefferson, and Madison had a radical vision of freedom."

— **Hal Lindsey**
Author of *The Late
Great
Planet Earth,*
Bestselling Book
of the Decade (1970s)

"For twenty-five years I have tried to get our fellow Americans to realize that the anti-God, anti-moral controllers of our media, education system, and entertainment industry are against America and the principles on which our God-fearing founders built the greatest country in the history of the world. In *Taking Back America*, Joseph Farah says it better than I did and offers a workable plan for reversing our nation's moral decay by getting our government leaders to realize that we, the majority, really want this to be 'One Nation Under God.'"

— **Tim LaHaye**
Author, Minister,
Educator

TAKING AMERICA

BACK

A Radical Plan to Revive Freedom, Morality, and Justice

JOSEPH FARAH

WND BOOKS

Nashville

A DIVISION OF THOMAS NELSON, INC.

www.ThomasNelson.com

Library of Congress Cataloging-in-Publication

Farah, Joseph.
    Taking America back : a radical plan to revive freedom, morality, and justice / Joseph Farah.
      p. cm.
    ISBN 0-7852-6392-6 (hardcover)
    1. United States—Social conditions—21st century. 2. United States—Politics and government—21st century. 3. United States—Moral conditions. I. Title.
HN65 .F37 2002
306'.0973—dc21

Printed in the United States of America

03 04 05 06 07 BVG 5 4 3 2 1

This book, like all I do in my life, is first and foremost dedicated to my Lord and Savior, Jesus of Nazareth.

But there are some mortals I would like to remember: my precious wife, Elizabeth, who is my inspiration, my reality check, my conscience, my teacher—not to mention the love of my life.

In a sense, this is not a dedication, but a daddy-cation. My hope is that my kids—Ashley, Alana, Alyssa, Kathleen, and Grace—will inherit an America that is better, freer, and more responsible than the one my generation helped destroy.

If and when they do, I trust they will find this book helpful in preserving the great gift they have received.

CONTENTS

INTRODUCTION

THIS BOOK IS A BATTLE CRY OF FREEDOM.

It's written from the heart—and from the gut.

Like the old town crier, I'm hoping to wake up Americans and give them the news. They've been asleep too long. They've been asleep at the switch. They've allowed their country to be stolen away from them while they slumbered.

I want it back. And I'm looking for a few good Americans to help me.

Oh, I know what some of you are going to say: "Farah, this is the greatest country on earth. What are you talking about?"

I can't dispute that statement, and I'm glad I can't. America is still the greatest country on earth. But that standard is not high enough for me. Is it the greatest country that it *has ever been?* No. America has seen better days. And there's a reason. We've sold out our principles, forgotten what made us great, settled for a phony kind of "safety and security," and left our freedom in the wake.

That's why it's time for Taking America Back.

As I wrote this book, there was a song playing in my head. It has become one of my inspirations.

In 1992, a friend of mine, singer-songwriter Steve Vaus, signed a recording contract with RCA. The resulting CD was called *We Must Take America Back*, and the title track instantly struck a chord with Americans starved for entertainment that spoke to them, touched their hearts, and reinforced their core values. In an age when performers are glorifying cop killers, drug use, and the abuse of women, it is the kind of music that sends chills down your spine:

> The American Dream has become a nightmare.
> Signs of the times are on cardboard on corners in town.
> There's a cancer called crime in our cities.
> And an unspoken fear we're on our way down.
>
> We must take America back:
> Put an end to the gangs and the drugs in the streets,
> And the fact that the bad guys most always go free,
> That is wrong.
> We need leaders who lead us, not stick us and bleed us,
> Then take all our money and send it abroad.
> We must take America back:
> We need prayer in the schools and more things
> Made in USA.
> It's the least we can do, for the red, white, and blue.
>
> We must take America back.
>
> There's a hell here on earth in some city schoolyards.
> When bullets and birth control outnumber books, something's wrong.
> There's a hunger for good news and heroes.
> But good news is no news so all of the heroes are gone.
>
> We must take America back.

The song began climbing the charts in some markets. Many radio stations found it was the most requested song in their inventory after listeners had a chance to hear it. Vaus's star seemed to be rising. But was RCA happy about its new artist's success? No. In fact, after a few complaints from some big-city radio stations about the patriotic nature of the song, the company decided to pull the CD off the market.

Thus, Steve Vaus's big-time entertainment-industry career was short-circuited. But it hardly stopped him. In fact, if anything, it made him more determined than ever to write and sing from his heart about the deteriorating state of his nation, the cultural morass, the political cowardice, the social engineering—and the way back.

There's a price to pay for doing what Steve Vaus has done. Besides being gagged by his record company, he's been targeted by threats and abused and harassed by the Internal Revenue Service.

It's time for all of us to take a stand as Steve Vaus did, not just in the voting booths, on the political soapboxes, and in the letters-to-the-editor columns, but behind the cultural barricades—where the real struggle for our nation's future is being waged by a handful of talented, gifted, and freedom-loving guerrilla fighters.

Just before beginning the writing of this book, Elizabeth and I moved close to Washington, D.C., from rural southern Oregon. A friend asked me why we would leave the beautiful, safe, surroundings of the redwood forest for Washington.

My answer? That's where the bad guys are.

It's time to take them on. It's time to challenge the status quo. It's time to rekindle the revolutionary spirit of our founders. It's time to take America back.

One acquaintance suggested that I might become corrupted by Washington, that it would "eat me alive."

My response? He that is in me is greater than he that dominates this city—a city I refer to as "the belly of the beast."

It may not be popular right now to refer to the nation's capital as the belly of the beast, but in a very real way it is accurate. Concentrations of power are always dangerous to liberty. And never before in the history of the world has more power been concentrated in one city than it is today in Washington, D.C.

Even though we are involved in what I consider to be a righteous and necessary war against Islamic terrorism in all its many manifestations, the real, long-term danger to America's freedom begins right here in Washington, where every day more laws are created than the people could possibly even read, let alone thoughtfully approve, let alone obey.

Bad decisions about how to spend your money are being made more frequently than ever before. Your personal freedoms are being compromised. Your heritage of liberty and self-government is being denied. Your rights to life, liberty, and property are being destroyed.

Never before in American history has a vigilant watchdog on government been more needed. But more than a watchdog is needed. We need Paul Reveres. We need Tom Paines. We need Washingtons and Jeffersons and Madisons. We need leaders who lead us, not stick us and bleed us.

Sure, I could have remained comfortable in the woods. My own freedom would be greater. My own safety would be more assured. But this is a time to challenge the status quo. This is a time for agitation. This is a time for hard work. This is a time for risks.

The battle lines have been drawn.

Americans are faced with an unresponsive and unaccountable one-party political system, an establishment propaganda machine posing as a free press, and cultural institutions (educational, charitable, entertainment, etc.) seduced by the materialist gods of the all-powerful secular state.

Let me speak plainly: The crisis we are in today cannot be resolved through the political system. It cannot be corrected by electing certain politicians to office. A much more profound, long-term, and fundamental shift is needed to right the U.S. ship of state.

What am I talking about?

America did not lose its freedom overnight. And we as Americans will not regain our freedom overnight.

Slowly but steadily over the last two hundred years, Americans have compromised the principles set forth by the founders in the Declaration of Independence and the Constitution. *Compromised* might not be the appropriate term—perhaps *sold out* would be more accurate.

Today, Americans live in a country the founders would scarcely recognize—not because of the automobiles speeding down freeways, nor because of the high-rise monuments full of paper pushers in our big cities, nor because of all the other technological advances we have made in the last two centuries. What would disappoint the founders is the fact that Americans have frittered away the freedom for which their forefathers fought and sacrificed.

That freedom, I am convinced, cannot be won back at the ballot box. The all-powerful state and its appendages in the influential cultural institutions that support it offer too much resistance. Just think of how the efforts of good men and women who go to Washington with the best intentions are thwarted and betrayed.

And it's getting worse all the time. What legacy will be left for your children? Your grandchildren? Do you think, the way America is going, that they will be as well-educated as you? Do you think they will be as moral? Will they be as safe as you? Will they have the opportunities to achieve, prosper, and excel that you had? The way America is going, do you think they will be as free as you?

Let's face it: America is on the decline—in almost every way. Look around you when you visit a major city and see vagrants huddled in alleyways. Look at what passes for entertainment on television. Look at the way our politicians in Washington disregard the law of the land and protect their own narrow interests rather than those of the people. Look at the threats on the horizon. Do you feel confident that the recent crop of leadership can handle them?

There have been many books outlining the problems America is facing. This book is different because it deals with solutions—radical solutions, revolutionary solutions, real solutions.

It's time for another revolution.

By that I do not mean it's time to organize armed militias and storm federal offices. Rather, it's time for revolutionary thinking, planning, education, and organizing. It's time to stop pretending we can change the course of the nation through "business as usual." It's time to wake up Americans to their plight. It's time to show them that there really are viable alternatives to serfdom—if not for us, maybe for our children.

Five years ago, my wife, Elizabeth, and I founded the Internet news site WorldNetDaily.com as a vehicle for igniting that kind of revolutionary thinking.

The Internet itself is revolutionary—perhaps even more so than the printing press was several hundred years ago. It was the pamphleteers, after all, who set the stage for the Continental Congress. Pamphleteers can't reach 300 million Americans very easily. But the New Media can—and does.

In the same way, my hope is that this book will reignite the torches of liberty across this great land.

It is written with three goals in mind:

- to remind us of the revolutionary creed of freedom and responsibility upon which this nation was founded;

- to show us how far we have fallen from that vision today; and

- to lay out a battle plan for reestablishing ourselves as an independent, self-governing people.

That's what this book is all about. It's about how to protect yourself and your family from the eroding culture, while simultaneously working to reclaim it, redeem it, restore it.

It's also about winning, not whining. It's about victory, not victimhood. It's about courage, not compromise.

It's truly about Taking America Back.

★ 1 ★

IMMORAL, FAT, LAZY, STUPID

A general Dissolution of Principles and Manners will more surely overthrow the Liberties of America than the whole force of the Common Enemy.

—SAMUEL ADAMS

I LOVE AMERICA.

I love the spacious skies.

I love the amber waves of grain, the purple mountains' majesty, and the fruited plains.

But what I love most about America is the God-breathed revolutionary spirit that led its founders to risk everything in a desperate fight for freedom and a noble effort to write the greatest Constitution the world has ever known.

However, something dreadful has happened to that spirit.

It's gone.

Oh, there's a small remnant of people who still have it, understand it, and live by it. But apparently the vast majority of Americans are clueless about it. They have no sense of history. They have no connection with their revolutionary past. They have no idea how blessed they are to live with even the fleeting legacy of freedom they inherited from

George Washington, Thomas Jefferson, James Madison, and our other forefathers who staked their lives, their fortunes, and their sacred honor in a quest for liberty.

They don't want to know what they can do for their country. They want to know what their country can do for them.

It's enough to make you sick.

Sure, Americans have lots of scapegoats for their ignorance. They've been deliberately dumbed down for thirty or more years by government schools determined to turn them into mindless robots. They have been the victims of media propaganda designed to deceive them and lead them astray. And for a generation or more they have been seduced by government into an ever-greater sense of dependency.

But those are excuses. The truth is out there. It's more readily available to Americans who choose to seek it than it has been for any other people in the history of the world. Americans are just too busy, blind, or comfortable to bother searching for it. Most don't even comprehend the way they are being manipulated—or just don't care. In other words, ultimately, we have no one to blame but ourselves.

We've lost our moorings. America is morally, politically, intellectually, and spiritually adrift. There are no anchors aboard. No compasses. The USS *America* is at the mercy of the winds and currents, and most on board don't care. As long as the crew is serving them fine food and entertaining them, the passengers don't give a second thought to their fate or their ultimate destination.

There's an iceberg ahead. It's called tyranny.

We must take America back before it's too late.

Let me tell you about a day when all of this hit me like a ton of bricks.

It was Independence Day—July 4, 1997. My wife, Elizabeth, and I decided to take the children to see the Statue of Liberty. What better place to celebrate the founding of the greatest nation in the world? Perhaps Independence Hall in Philadelphia? Maybe, but we were in New York—and this would be an opportunity to teach our kids about the ideals of freedom upon which the American Dream was created.

The first surprise was how few people would be joining us for this 221st anniversary of the signing of the Declaration of Independence. The ferry ride over to Ellis Island and then Liberty Island was beautiful; the sun was shining and the breeze was blowing. But only a handful of Americans were making the trek with us. And many of those were foreigners, speaking other languages, but clearly in awe of the vision of Thomas Jefferson and the courage of the patriots who stood with him against tyranny, religious persecution, and oppressive taxation.

On Ellis Island we quickly found the wall commemorating the arrival of millions of immigrants who came to this country early in the twentieth century and contributed so much to building the world's most benevolent superpower. The names of my paternal grandmother, Alexandra Kurdock, and grandfather, Joseph Farah, were etched upon that wall. I reflected upon their own courage in making those long, lonely journeys from Middle Eastern countries in search of freedom and opportunity. I tried to give my girls a sense of what their ancestors must have endured to give them the relatively comfortable life we all now take for granted.

Though I grew up in the New York area, I had never made this simple trip before. The statue was more beautiful than I had ever imagined. What a sight it must have been for those immigrants as they made their way to Ellis Island.

As a remembrance of this special day, we took the children to the island's official gift shop, run by the U.S. Park Service. Inside we purchased several replicas of the statue and historical reference works on the mammoth task of building it and restoring it to its present glory. The kids were as excited as their parents about their new treasures, which would occupy a place of honor in our home.

But what a shock and disappointment for their parents when we examined the prizes more closely and found three incredible words stamped on the bottom: "Made in China."

This was symbolism so tragic—so ironic—that it quickly brought us back to the reality of what we as a nation are facing today.

Think about it. At least two thousand Chinese citizens risked their lives only a few short years ago in Tiananmen Square for the grave offense of erecting a papier-mâché replica of this symbol of liberty and individual rights. The Chinese government ruthlessly stormed the crowd of freedom-loving protesters and smashed that statue. Now, apparently, the U.S. Park Service has contracted with a Chinese company to make tiny replicas for tourists visiting the Statue of Liberty!

We thought long and hard about the poor Chinese workers—some perhaps in slave labor camps—toiling away their hours and days making little Statues of Liberty while they themselves would never have the chance to experience the promise it represents.

Contemporary China is the very antithesis of everything for which the founding fathers fought and died. Religious persecution worse than any they ever experienced or imagined is taking place today in this "enlightened" age in modern China. The slavery with which they wrestled so long ago and over which we as a nation shed so much blood and abolished nearly 150 years ago still persists in China. Grotesque human rights abuses—including forced abortions and severe state-imposed limitations on childbirth—are a way of life. Freedom of expression and freedom of the press are unheard of in present-day China.

I wondered, *Has America sold its very soul?*

Part of me wanted to tear that "Made in China" label off those little statues. But I think we'll leave them alone. We'll use them as a way to teach our kids about how fragile freedom really is. We'll leave them as a constant reminder that none of us are truly free as long as some of us are deprived of our God-given rights.

Someday soon, though, I want to see such trinkets made in America again. I want to awaken this country so that no government agency would ever consider contracting with a hostile foreign slave power to produce replicas of the Statue of Liberty. I want to create a climate in this country—an awareness—that would never tolerate the sale of such merchandise at a national monument.

I doubt anyone else even gave the "Made in China" label a second thought that July day in 1997. That's what really bothered me. That's what got me thinking about a Second American Revolution. That's what got me concerned about how Americans are out to sea without a rudder. Clueless.

Psychic and material comfort is the only standard by which Americans today measure their lives, their liberty, and their pursuits of happiness. Wal-Mart's shelves are laden with Chinese goods. They are cheaper than those made in the U.S.—if you can even find any made in the U.S., if you even care enough to look.

How did we get to this point?

I'm not a conspiracy nut. Yet I've come to the conclusion that there is a conspiracy of sorts at work in America today.

I don't pretend to know who is directing it. I don't fully understand how it works. And for the life of me I can't figure out why Americans permit themselves to be manipulated by it.

Nevertheless, it's time to expose it. It's time to break its stranglehold on our nation. It's time to undo the damage it has wrought on us and set America back on course.

What is this grand conspiracy that is destroying the very fiber of our once-free republic?

It's a plot to make the American people immoral, fat, lazy, and stupid. And it's working. Every day, it seems, Americans are a little less righteous, a little less lean, a little less energetic and motivated, and a lot less intelligent. How else do we explain the following:

The government now taxes the most productive Americans at rates approaching 50 percent. The wealth it forcefully confiscates from a minority of productive citizens is then redistributed in various ways mainly designed to create a permanent subculture of dependency—and thus a ready supply of votes to ensure reelection of incumbent politicians.

The government ignores strict, specific, and clear constitutional limitations on its power—spending almost nothing on meaningful defense of the American people, the main reason for a federal government, and hundreds of billions on programs and giveaways that would make our founding fathers spin in their graves.

The government invents phony environmental crises—like "global warming," ozone depletion, CFCs, "endangered" species, etc. Ignoring the fact that private property ownership and free enterprise have proven to be the best models for conservation and stewardship, the government uses these issues to monopolize power, centralize authority, and attack individual liberty and personal responsibility.

The government has abrogated its responsibility to maintain national sovereignty by illegally granting international agencies and bodies authority over U.S. law and the Constitution.

The government is undermining even such basic constitutionally guaranteed rights as free speech with restrictive campaign laws limiting the way we as Americans can use our resources, our time, and our money to effect political change. Never before in American history has there been such a blatant move to safeguard the political status quo through manipulation of the electoral process.

The government has abdicated its constitutional authority to coin money and handed over decisions about printing paper money, not backed by gold or silver, to an unaccountable private cartel of bankers known as the Federal Reserve.

The government is quickly adding sexual deviants to the list of protected classes of people. In other words, it will soon be a crime across the board to draw conclusions about people based on their behavior. What on earth are we supposed to use as criteria for making judgments about people if not behavior?

The government considers the aborting of innocent unborn children a natural right. Yet there is widespread debate still about whether the death penalty for convicted murderers is "cruel and unusual punishment."

The government penalizes—with a special, onerous tax—married people, thereby encouraging couples to shack up instead of making a lifelong commitment.

The government discourages at every turn, through strict regulation of churches and church-related ministries, the civic involvement of pastors, priests, and rabbis—the very people to whom officials should willingly turn for moral counseling and guidance.

Even in the wake of the devastating September 11 terrorist attacks on American citizens, the government has demonstrated its unwillingness to trust, empower, and rally the one precious resource that can bring us victory over our foreign and domestic enemies—the people themselves. As of this writing, even airline pilots are denied the right to carry firearms to protect themselves, their passengers, and their crews. The government builds up a new bureaucracy as the answer to the crisis rather than leading the people in an effort to protect themselves.

I could go on and on, but you get the picture. Government is intentionally encouraging and spreading immorality. Government is intentionally depriving the American people of self-government. Government is intentionally destroying the legacy of freedom established by our founding fathers and enshrined in our Declaration of Independence and Constitution. Government is turning us into slaves.

But it gets worse, I'm afraid.

Government is just part of the problem. The very soul of America has been infected. The culture has lost its moral bearings. Society can no longer tell right from wrong. The civilization itself is becoming something less than civil.

This, too, is part of a deliberate plot.

After all, politicians do not lead; they follow. They do not stand up to the tremendous pressures applied by the cultural and political establishment. They bend. They compromise. They yield. It is unusual for a politician to place principle over personal ambition. And that's how the freedom stealers win battle after battle.

It's the culture, stupid. For those who are old enough to remember the Vietnam War, here's an analogy: The culture is the Ho Chi Minh trail to political power. And the culture has been deliberately used and abused to transform our political system, to change the way Americans think, to attack our values, to demean our faith in God, to reduce that shining city on a hill to the status of a drab public housing project.

It all started about a hundred years ago, around the turn of the century, when an Italian Communist by the name of Antonio Gramsci came up with a strategic spin on accomplishing the political objectives of socialism. Gramsci argued that the road to victory wasn't necessarily found in armed, violent clashes, but rather in a long-term struggle for the hearts and minds of the people.

He advocated a long march through the cultural institutions—education, academia, the press, the entertainment industry, the foundations, even the churches. If you take over the key cultural institutions, he said, the political establishment would fall into your hands like the last domino.

The enemies of freedom, the advocates of state control and socialism, have been following Gramsci's cue around the world for at least the last seventy-five years.

They have thoroughly succeeded in sacking America's cultural institutions—and, today, the political establishment is sitting there like an overripe plum waiting to be harvested.

Let me give you an example. From the 1930s through the mid-1960s, the churches, both Catholic and Protestant, wielded enormous clout in Hollywood. Clergy and laymen representing both branches of Christianity literally approved every script made into a motion picture by the major studios until 1968. At that time, the churches voluntarily relinquished this powerful influence they had over America's culture.

Why? Not because there was any pressure from the film industry. In fact, Hollywood moguls begged the churches to stay involved. They understood it was good for business. The involvement of the churches helped ensure that Hollywood produced films that would be well received by the vast mainstream audience. Left to their own devices, the studio heads understood they could easily lose touch—that artistic license could easily lead to licentiousness. Yet I doubt any of them could have imagined how quickly the entertainment industry would plummet into the moral abyss. The result? Two-thirds of all movies today are rated R. Fewer people go to movies today than did after World War II. Only skyrocketing ticket prices, video rentals, and television distribution have kept the industry rolling in profits. But is there anyone who doubts Hollywood would be better off, making higher profits, if it was still producing movies as it did in its "golden age"?

Why did the church abandon Hollywood? Because social activists who had penetrated the church as part of that long-range strategy devised by Gramsci engineered the move. There is simply no other explanation. At the time, the National Council of Churches, which oversaw the Protestant Film Office, claimed it could no longer afford to monitor scripts. The influence the churches had on Hollywood and the broader American culture cost a grand total of $35,000 a year when the office was closed.

Today the National Council of Churches is at the forefront of every statist social cause under the sun. Closing the film office was merely the first volley in a long war against freedom, personal responsibility, and self-government.

Think of the way the movies have changed in the last generation— from *Beach Blanket Bingo* to *Natural Born Killers*. Think of the way television has changed—from *Father Knows Best* to *Temptation Island*. The popular culture has become a moral cesspool overflowing with toxic sludge that seeps into the souls of innocent kids. There's no protecting them if they have any contact with their peers.

It's painful even to think about the effect of the popular culture on kids, and even more difficult to imagine it's the same story in every city and town across America—every day, every week, for years. There's no escape. What impact do such images leave on impressionable minds? What damage do they inflict on young hearts? What scars do they leave on their souls?

When I was a kid, TV was wholesome. It may have been idiotic at times, but my parents didn't have to worry about what I watched. And mostly I watched baseball games.

I still like to watch baseball—especially in October when every game counts. And now I like to watch baseball with my kids— explaining every play, the strategy, the history, the personalities and individual talents of players.

But I find that I can't even watch baseball games with my kids without being bombarded by inappropriate and offensive advertising.

It's really incredible—and sad.

It doesn't matter whether it's NBC or Fox, CBS or ESPN, I find I am increasingly uncomfortable during commercial time. I've had to endure rather explicit Pfizer ads for Viagra and other products dealing with erectile dysfunction. I've had to endure spot after spot for the NBC comedy *Friends,* in which every scene seems to have someone jumping on top of another person or reacting to sexual innuendo. I've had to endure endless promotions for another show focusing on the exploits of a young vixen sleeping with a father-son combo.

I could go on and on, but you get the idea. Welcome to prime time in the twenty-first century.

Do you think government will help you? Forget about it. The federal government, remember, is responsible for even the worse taste—sponsoring obscenity and pornography in the name of art and paying for political propaganda and calling it news. Please, people, don't think you are going to get any help from Washington. Washington is a bigger problem than Hollywood—really it is.

But it is time for Americans to stand up and be counted for propriety, for basic decency, for virtue, for self-restraint, for morality, for goodness, and for heaven's sake, yes, for the children.

Ratings systems are not the answer. We should have learned that lesson from the movie industry. It's simply time to demand accountability and responsibility.

For those of us who believe in the marketplace, this is the only way to go.

It's also time to return to what has worked in the past.

Prior to the institution of the ratings system by the Motion Picture Association of America, the film industry maintained its moral bearings through a close relationship with U.S. churches. The Catholic and Protestant Churches voluntarily, at the behest of the major studios, reviewed scripts and (when needed) advised content changes and suggested cuts.

Hollywood loved this relationship. It guaranteed that its products would be well received by the churchgoing American public, families, and children, the biggest possible audiences. Far more people attended movies during the thirty years of this system than in the thirty years since. Far more. The result—creatively speaking—was Hollywood's "golden age" of movies.

But then the churches walked out.

In the vacuum that followed—and in a desperate effort to maintain some standards for the creative community, which always pushes the envelope on moral themes and artistic license—the MPAA developed the movie ratings system in 1968.

The effect of the ratings system was to give parents a sense of complacency about the content of movies. Parents didn't pay attention to what their kids were seeing, probably believing—falsely—that their kids would be kept out of theaters showing R-rated movies. Anyone who has attended an R-rated movie lately knows that unsupervised kids are plentiful in those theaters. It's frightening when you consider the themes and graphic images to which they are exposed.

Hollywood directors have shirked any sense of responsibility since the ratings system began. They have a built-in excuse: "I'm making an adult movie, not one for kids. After all, it will be rated R. Just keep your kids out." That's what they say, yet most of these R-rated movies are intentionally made for teenagers—boys in particular.

Now the same misguided principle—one that clearly didn't work— is being applied to television.

Since the ratings system began, television content has plummeted to new lows. And it's not just a question of stopping your own kids from watching the filth. What about your neighbors' kids? How do you exercise any influence over them? And how will you prevent them from influencing *your* kids—or worse yet, victimizing them?

You can place your kids in private schools; you can take away their television sets; you can monitor the kind of music they listen to, but it is next to impossible in America today to shelter them from nasty, immoral, unhealthy, dangerously destructive cultural influences. And it is impossible to protect them from the other members of society who choose to live in that polluted moral ecosystem.

What is needed to reclaim the culture is a reemphasis on personal responsibility—not just by parents and kids, but by the entertainment industry as well. The purveyors of garbage need to rediscover shame—not under government coercion, but under pressure from the marketplace.

That's how Culture War is waged. As Hollywood demonstrates, dropping out isn't the answer. The answer is for freedom-loving people to fight back on all fronts, to stop surrendering in the Culture War, to reclaim and redeem those lost cultural institutions.

I believe God will bless such a campaign. After all, the enemies of freedom are the enemies of God. They declared war on Him and the whole notion of a sovereign Supreme Being when they set out on their destructive path to empower the state as the ultimate authority. But God still sits on the throne. He's still in charge. His Spirit is far more powerful than any worldly forces.

It reminds me of the words of the revolutionary naval hero John Paul Jones as his foundering ship was besieged and bombarded by the British fleet: "I have not yet begun to fight."

That's the spirit that will carry the day. That's the spirit that will be empowered and rewarded by God.

That pressure can only be turned up to high by one institution—the same religious bodies that abandoned responsibility for the culture a generation ago. They need to reengage. They need to reassert themselves, their values, and their ethics. In short, they need to redefine right and wrong for a culture hopelessly adrift in a sea of moral relativism.

The American people are not going to rise up spontaneously to reverse this moral slide. America has lost respect for innocence, for childhood itself. Certainly no government policy is likely to restore that—though I can think of many that have contributed to the problem. No system of voluntary ratings by an industry run by immature, unaccountable, unprincipled egomaniacs can hope to return our society to virtuousness.

How do we fight back?

That's what this book is all about. It's a blueprint for taking our country back, piece by piece, one day at a time, one battle at a time.

Fighting back means confrontation. In this case it means talking to the children who are no more than victims of this insanity. It means asking theater managers why they are allowing underage children to attend such movies. And yes, it even means confronting parents with their own shameful irresponsibility. Each individual action may seem too insignificant to trifle with, yet as Edmund Burke said, "The only thing necessary for the triumph of evil is for good men to do nothing."

It also means talking to your pastor, your rabbi, or your priest, encouraging and prodding them to reengage the culture.

Today, nothing short of a general cultural reawakening—a spiritual revival, if you will—can save us from ourselves. All of us, not just Washington and Hollywood, need constant reminding that there are indeed moral absolutes in this universe of ours. There are right ways and wrong ways of behaving and, especially, of rearing children. There are immutable laws that have worked pretty well for nearly six thousand years. Ignore them, as we have recently, and the world goes to hell in a handcart.

Our only hope is to stop ignoring the corrosive evil that surrounds us. Confront it. Battle it. Defeat it.

It can be done. It must be done.

It's time to take America back.

Just think about the goal every time you are confronted with evil.

Are you ready to give up on America?

Are you ready to abandon the legacy of Washington, Jefferson, and Madison?

Are you ready to walk away from your responsibility to God to do what is right?

That's the problem with taking even one more step down the slippery slope of moral relativism. There is no way back.

Over and over again in the Bible we see what happens when the people "do what is right in their own eyes," forgetting the only rules that really mean anything—those given to us by God.

We can forget all that. We can disregard it. We can chalk it all up to legend, myth, and superstition. But we do so at our own risk.

It's time for everyone to choose what kind of world they would like to live in. The choice is simple: the world of standards and morality, of marriage, order, the rule of law, and accountability to God? Or the world of anything-goes, aberrant sexual behavior; do-your-own-thing lifestyles; and moral codes that change with the speed of the latest public-opinion poll?

Now I've explained to you how Americans have become immoral, but what about fat, lazy, and stupid?

Have you visited a government school lately? I won't dwell here on the intentional dumbing down that is so obvious it can only be deliberate. Now, faced with decades of declining test scores and rampant functional illiteracy among high-school students and graduates, the National Education Association—which virtually dictates federal education policy—is calling for more emphasis in the classroom on teaching "alternative lifestyles." I kid you not.

But immorality and stupidity are not the only end products of the government educational system—not by a long shot.

Fat and lazy people are by-products as well.

I don't know if you have noticed, but physical education is no longer a serious part of the government school curriculum in most districts. Now, "gym," as it was once called, is coed—meaning boys and girls are supposed to hone their athletic skills and workouts together. Of course, as any grown-up should be able to predict, such a program turns the high-school phys ed hour into the high-school sexual politics hour. What's next? Coed showers?

Have you noticed how overweight our children are today? Thirty years ago you could count on one fat kid in every classroom. That's what I remember from my own experience in school. Today, the reverse is usually true.

So, there you have it—Americans are being bred by their government to be immoral, fat, lazy, and stupid.

But why? Why would the government want Americans to be immoral, fat, lazy, and stupid?

Think about it, now. I'll give you a moment.

OK, time's up.

Here's the answer: It comes in the form of a quote from one of the great American founders—one often underappreciated among a long list of heroes who are underappreciated. His name was Samuel Adams, and here's what he said that answers the question of why the power brokers in Washington would want a nation of immoral, fat, lazy, and stupid people to govern:

> A general Dissolution of Principles and Manners will more surely overthrow the Liberties of America than the whole force of the Common Enemy. While the People are virtuous they cannot be subdued; but when once they lose their Virtue they will be ready to surrender their Liberties to the first external or internal invader . . . If Virtue and Knowledge are diffused among the People, they will never be enslaved. This will be their great Security.

Now, I don't expect any immoral, fat, lazy, and stupid people to comprehend that profound statement. But for those of you moral, lean, enterprising, and intelligent people out there, this learned, insightful statement provides the motive for the madness we see around us.

We're a nation of fat, stupid cattle being led to slaughter by an internal invader—our own government—which is no longer the servant of a self-governing people. It has become the master, the governor of a people incapable and unwilling to govern themselves.

Is this situation hopeless? No.

Is the situation grave? Yes.

Is there much time left for those of us who recognize it to switch gears and get our nation back on track?

No.

Will we take America back?

You bet.

Just like the cultural Marxists took a long march through the institutions to conquer them one by one, let's begin our march to win them back.

It's time to ignite the Second American Revolution. It's time to celebrate virtue and knowledge again. It's time to wake up your neighbors so they can once again smell the sweet aroma of freedom.

Are you with me?

Let's take America back.

Read on.

★ 2 ★

THE SECOND AMERICAN REVOLUTION

The tree of liberty must be refreshed from time to time with the blood of patriots and tyrants. It is its natural manure.

—THOMAS JEFFERSON

IF WE'RE EVER GOING TO MAKE THE U.S. GOVERN-
ment responsive to the will of the people, it's going to take a revolution.

I don't necessarily mean a violent, armed clash between patriots who still believe in self-government and the forces of the U.S. Defense Department. But I do mean a real revolution. Nothing short of that can save us from tyranny, despotism, and slavery. It's just a matter of time.

Thomas Jefferson understood that we'd need a revolution every twenty years or so to keep government in check.

Even one hundred years later, President Theodore Roosevelt saw what was happening to America—how it was sliding down what is a familiar road to students of history:

"The Roman Republic fell, not because of the ambition of Caesar or Augustus, but because it had already long ceased to be in any real sense a republic at all," said Roosevelt. He continued:

When the sturdy Roman plebian, who lived by his own labor, who voted without reward according to his own convictions, and who with his fellows joined in war the terrible Roman legion, had been changed into an idle creature who craved nothing in life save the gratification of a thirst for vapid excitement, who was fed by the state, and who directly or indirectly sold his vote to the highest bidder, then the end of the republic was at hand, and nothing could save it. The laws were the same as they had been, but the people behind the laws had changed, and so the laws counted for nothing.

Does that sound familiar? Does it sound like modern America?

The Constitution is today little more than a historical relic. The basis for the rule of law in America has been twisted and perverted beyond recognition. The document once understood by farmers, ranchers, and other ordinary people is now interpreted by lawyers and judges to mean, in many cases, just the opposite of what it says.

In its place we have tens of thousands of federal laws, rules, and regulations that no one can understand. No one could possibly have the time to read them—not even the lawyers who have to specialize in particular fields just to be proficient. So what's the point? The point is to set traps. There's an expression in America that goes like this: "If the government wants to get you, it will get you." Have you heard that? Do you agree with it? Have you seen evidence of it yourself?

It's true. If you make enemies with the powers that be in America, you could find yourself under special scrutiny. You could find many of those arcane laws being applied to you—unequally, of course, but who cares about equality under the law anymore?

That's what all those laws are for. They are there to show you who's boss. They empower government. They create make-work jobs, and those jobs create an even larger power base for the politicians who passed the laws. It's a vicious cycle that is sending our country swirling into the abyss of unaccountable tyranny.

I know what you're wondering: Who's going to lead the revolution?

Who's going to participate? How are Americans going to be awakened to the threats?

It's true that too many of the American people have been bought off—by comfort, by complacency, by *busyness,* as opposed to *business,* by disinformation, by manipulation, and by a process of deliberate dumbing down in a government-run educational system and by a semiofficial corporate media establishment. They've traded freedom for a false sense of security. What a bargain!

But revolutions are rarely successfully waged by a majority of the people. That wasn't the case in 1776. And it won't be the case in the twenty-first century.

I've heard that the Bolshevik Revolution in Russia succeeded when only 3 percent of the people were members of the Communist Party. Three percent. Does our remnant of self-aware, self-governing, responsible, free men and women total 3 percent in America? I think so.

Don't pass the buck. It's up to you. Don't wait for leaders to emerge; become one. Rise up in righteous anger. Rise up in righteous indignation. Rise up in righteous determination.

You can do it. Your forefathers did it. This is your destiny.

Nothing short of revolution can save us now.

What do I mean by "revolution"?

I mean people must once again take control of their government—not beginning with their elected representatives in Washington, but right in their own backyards. The focus needs to be on town councils, school boards, county commissions, planning boards, zoning boards, etc.

That's where the next great rebellion must start. If self-governing citizens cannot demand accountability at that level, there is little hope of expecting it from members of Congress. And there is little hope of greater victories that would fundamentally redefine the scope of Washington's authority over our lives.

Such a rebellion is under way in a few places in America. One great example is Klamath Falls, Oregon, a sleepy rural area on the border of two states known for their advanced stages of socialism and top-down style of "We-know-better-than-you" government. When the federal government shut off supplies of water to ranchers and farmers in the area in an effort to preserve some supposedly endangered fish, freedom-loving people traveled from three different states in a "convoy of tears" to bring supplies and donations.

The locals also defied federal authorities and turned the water back on. Civil disobedience? Yes and no. Because the federal government has no legitimate jurisdiction in the states and local communities. It wasn't really lawbreaking. The federal government is breaking the law—defying the Constitution of the United States by meddling in affairs not of its concern. But it does take courage—no matter what you call it.

The organizers of this rebellion recognize they are in a war—a war of ideas, a war of lifestyles, a war of philosophy, a war of world visions, a war of spiritual dimensions, and a war every bit as real and important as the War for Independence launched in 1776.

It's a war that won't be won if we try to wage it only through letters to our congressmen. It's a war that won't be won by electing the right officials in Washington. It's a war that won't be won only by complaining. But it is a war that can be won if people recognize the problem and begin acting at the local level—as the heroes of Klamath Falls are doing.

In other parts of the country, local sheriffs and county commissioners are telling the federal government where to get off—literally. They are chasing out U.S. Fish and Wildlife officials. They are escorting Environmental Protection Agency bureaucrats out of their jurisdictions. They are even telling the FBI and the Bureau of Alcohol, Tobacco, and Firearms to take a hike.

And they are succeeding. Why? Because the federal government doesn't want a war with popular local movements. The Feds would prefer to take on the unpopular movements—those that are harder to understand. That's why they were able to burn down the Branch Davidian Church in Waco, Texas, and kill every man, woman, and child inside without accountability.

So the number one way to bring on the revolution is to take control of your local town council, your local police department, and your local school district. When you begin challenging federal authority, the revolution is under way.

It's time for people to awaken to the grave threats to our liberties. It's not a time to stand still. It's a time to go on the offensive, just as our founders did.

This kind of struggle is beyond the two major political institutions and ideologies at work in America today. This is not about Democrats versus Republicans or conservatives versus liberals.

I'm not a conservative, and I'm certainly no liberal—at least in the way that term is defined today. This comes as a shock to some people. We have come to view politics in America in this paradigm of right or left, conservative or liberal, Republican or Democrat. I tell you that is no choice at all.

I don't like the label "conservative." I reject the label. With all due respect to my "conservative" friends, I find the description detestable, extremely unflattering, simplistic, and an insult.

Let me tell you why.

Conservatives, by definition, seek to conserve something from the past—institutions, cultural mores, values, political beliefs, traditions. What happens when a society moves so far from righteous values and freedom principles that there is little left to conserve?

That is where I believe America finds itself in the early part of the twenty-first century. Let me give you some examples of why:

- the breakdown of the institutions of marriage and the family

- the inability of many to distinguish between right and wrong

- the consolidation of power in Washington and in the executive branch

- the breakdown in the rule of law

- the usurpation of power by unaccountable supranational agencies

- infringements on personal freedoms

- increasing vulnerability to weapons of mass destruction, and government's unwillingness or inability to address such a basic concept of defense

What do these and other problems our nation is facing have in common?

Today we have a federal government that acts without regard for the Constitution. What's the conservative prescription for that? Has "compassionate conservative" George W. Bush reversed unconstitutional government? No, he's continued it. It turns out "compassionate conservatism" is nothing more than "politically correct conservatism."

When political terms are so badly compromised that they no longer have meaning for people—at least not accurate meanings—then it's time to abandon them. Thomas Jefferson might have considered himself a liberal. But he was no liberal by today's standards. That term has been co-opted to mean something quite different than it formerly did.

And that's true of conservatism too.

Can you defeat unconstitutional government by putting your fingers in the dike to prevent more breaches? No, it takes a radical agenda to defeat a radical agenda. Conservatives have no stomach for fighting—the kind of fighting it takes to restore real freedom to America.

It's not a time for timidity or compromise. It's not a time for defensiveness and conciliation. It's time to take the offensive in this struggle.

I'm not a "conservative," because I see precious little left in this world worth conserving. Conservatives, from my experience, do not make good freedom fighters. They seem to think a victory is holding back attacks on liberty or minimizing them. They are forever on the defensive—trying to conserve or preserve an apple that is rotten to the core.

What is the rotten apple? You can see it in the government schools that dumb down American kids. You can see it in the universities that pervert the concepts of knowledge and wisdom. You can see it in the federalization and militarization of law enforcement. You can see it in the proliferation of nonconstitutional government. You can see it in the real "trickle-down economics" of confiscatory taxes. You can see it in the unaccountable authorities that give us global treaties. You can see it in the relentless attacks on marriage and the family. You can see it in euthanasia, population control, and the phony "right" to abortion on demand. You can see it in the surrender of our national security.

It's all got to go. But how? Politics as usual will never get us there.

Conservatives, it seems to me, only forestall the inevitable slide into tyranny. I don't want to forestall it. I want to prevent it. I want to reverse that slide. I want to restore the dream that was America.

Was George Washington a conservative? No. He was a revolutionary. He is known throughout the world—or was when people appreciated such concepts—as the "father of freedom."

Today, those who stand for freedom, justice, the rule of law, self-government, and the moral principles of the Bible are not part of "the establishment." We're the rebels. By the world's standards we're the renegades.

What about libertarianism? Is that the best description of what I'm talking about?

Nope. That dog won't hunt, either.

Here's why I am not a libertarian—and why I believe that political movement will never resonate with the American people.

I believe a nation's borders are sacrosanct. Without borders, there are no nations. We become one big global village—subject ultimately to a new form of tyranny imposed by unaccountable internationalists. Borders are also critical to maintaining the distinct culture of a nation. That's not a racist or jingoistic concept—it is a matter of practicality. If anyone and everyone can become an American simply by relocating—and without any pledge to our nation's Constitution and political creed—then we lose everything our founding fathers established in fighting for our independence, our sovereignty, and for the rule of law.

While I agree with libertarians that our national drug laws and the enforcement of those laws are terribly abusive and beyond the scope of our Constitution, I have no problem with states and local governments passing laws prohibiting the sale of narcotics and enforcing such laws. The truth is, legalizing dangerous drugs will surely lead to increased use and abuse—a trend that could pose problems as severe or worse than those created by the drug war. I'm all for ending the drug war at the ineffective federal level, but condoning drug use is the wrong prescription.

America needs a strong defense—and this is a reality many libertarians don't accept. True, the concept of defense in America has been distorted and twisted. We spend megabillions not on defense, but on *offense*. We deploy tens of thousands of troops in more than a hundred countries around the world, as if America was the world's policeman. That is wrong. We leave Americans at home virtually defenseless against terrorist attacks and weapons of massive destruction. That is equally wrong.

Libertarians, more often than not, fail to understand the moral dimension so critical to self-government. Read the words of the founders. They all got it. They all intuitively understood that even the best form of representative and limited government would be twisted into coercive tyranny if the people did not have the basic morality necessary to govern themselves.

Libertarians make a fundamental mistake about the nature of man. Man is not inherently good. Man can only learn to govern himself when he understands there is a higher accountability—a higher authority. Ideally, that higher authority is not the government, but God. Government can only demand good behavior through force. But when individuals understand they are accountable to God, and that He requires certain kinds of behavior as defined in the Ten Commandments and the totality of Scripture, there is a chance for man to maximize his freedom here on earth.

Freedom can only be experienced and maximized, though, when it is accompanied by personal responsibility. Personal responsibility cannot be legislated. It cannot be forced. It cannot be coerced. Libertarians generally understand this, but too few of them comprehend that a *laissez-faire* society can only be built in a culture of morality, righteousness, and compassion.

Libertarians who expect to build such a society through politics alone make a fundamental error. In a sense, they are utopian dreamers like the socialists, ignoring the importance of human nature in shaping communities and nations.

I don't want to be too hard on the libertarians because, of all the political activists in America, they may have the best concept of limited constitutional government. That's a big start—but it's only a start. We cannot ignore the flaws in their positions. We cannot ignore the fact that they don't have a complete picture. We cannot ignore that a libertarian society devoid of God and a biblical worldview would quickly deteriorate into chaos and violence.

Would this country be better off with more libertarians? Absolutely. Do they have all the answers? Not even close.

The fact of the matter is there's more to life than politics. Much more. Here's the way George Washington put it in his inaugural address:

> The foundations of our national policy will be laid in the pure and immutable principles of private morality, and the preeminence of free government be exemplified by all the attributes which can win the affections of its citizens, and command the respect of the world. I dwell on this prospect with every satisfaction which an ardent love for my country can inspire: since there is no truth more thoroughly established, than that there exists in the economy and course of nature, an indissoluble union between virtue and happiness; between duty and advantage; between the genuine maxims of an honest and magnanimous policy, and the solid rewards of public prosperity and felicity: since we ought to be no less persuaded that the propitious smiles of Heaven can never be expected on a nation that disregards the external rules of order and right, which Heaven itself has ordained: and since the preservation of the sacred fire of liberty, and the destiny of the republican model of government, are justly considered as deeply, perhaps as finally, staked on the experiment entrusted to the hands of the American People.

When the libertarians adopt this sentiment, let me know. I'll be happy to consider the new label.

The founding fathers knew that even the best-designed government wouldn't work if the people were not righteous, moral, and God-fearing—if they didn't love liberty and cherish it. To practice self-government again, we must have a people capable of self-government.

It takes courage to stand in the gap, to man the barricades, to say "Enough is enough"—and mean it. It takes more than a "conservative" vision to lead the way back to freedom.

What about liberalism? What's wrong with liberalism? Liberalism, depending on how you define it, is *the* problem in America. Liberalism as we know it in the United States is an evil ideology inflicting massive suffering, misery, injustice, oppression, and death wherever it gains power and influence.

You might notice in my daily column and elsewhere that I never use *liberal* (or *liberalism*) as an epithet. I rarely use the term at all because I believe it is a misnomer and a label that is widely misunderstood. But for the purposes of this brief explanation of the various competing ideologies in America today, I am going to critique liberalism just as I critiqued conservatism and libertarianism.

Liberalism is the dominant ideology in Washington, D.C., today—no matter which political party runs the White House or Congress. Liberalism controls the Republican Party only to a slightly lesser degree than it controls the Democrats.

Liberalism proffers that it is a good idea to forcibly take the wealth and property rightfully and legally acquired by one party and redistribute it to others. Of course, liberals always take a sizable cut of the transaction for themselves—sometimes as much as 80 percent.

My friend columnist-economist Walter Williams accurately describes this process as "legalized theft." There is no better way to explain it. Legalized theft is the central creed of liberalism. Liberalism is not possible without it. All manner of justifications and rationalizations are made for this process—the greater good, helping the poor, leveling the playing field. No matter what you call it, theft is theft.

But theft is only the beginning of the evil that liberals spread.

Liberalism also kills. It kills in a thousand different ways. Let me give you a few:

Since the 1973 *Roe v. Wade* Supreme Court ruling, more than 30 million unborn babies have been killed in America. Liberals, in general, seem to have more respect and reverence for bald-eagle eggs than unborn humans.

By actively working to disarm the American population, in direct violation of the U.S. Constitution, liberals condemn the defenseless to death—often at the hands of criminals they help spring from prison.

Through opposition to missile defense and civil defense, liberals leave the entire civilian population open to annihilation at the hands of a nuclear-armed madman, an accidental launch by a nuclear power, or terrorist attacks.

Through overdeployment of the armed forces all over the world and wars like Vietnam, liberals kill U.S. soldiers, foreign soldiers, and civilians without a care about the constitutional basis for their actions.

Liberalism is less an ideology than utopian wishful thinking. It cares not about the actual results of its policies, only about doing something. The "something" that it does always empowers government at the expense of people.

Liberalism today is simply a new name for an old-fashioned idea formerly known as socialism. It stands on its head the basic concept of liberty as the founders thought of it. Liberals think the government that governs most governs best.

The sheer volume of laws it passes is staggering. No one has the time to read them, much less live by them. Yet each new law is another nail in the coffin of a free society.

Liberalism believes government is the best vehicle for solving problems—not the worst, not the course of last resort.

Government is the god of liberalism. And that's why I am in no danger of being mistaken for one. My god *is* God. How about yours?

I ask because, while I have been critical of the American people for losing their way, some surveys indicate they do not trust government nearly as much as their tolerance of it might suggest.

In 1997 the Pew Research Center for People and the Press asked a random sampling of Americans which groups and institutions they most trusted. The results received scant attention in the establishment press—not surprising given how few people trust the media as an institution. Only 22 percent said they had a lot of trust in their local daily newspapers. Only a slightly larger group, 24 percent, trusted local television news.

But for would-be revolutionaries of the twenty-first century, there is much more to this survey that needs to be analyzed. A third of this polling group said they trust their public schools—or as I call it, the government school monopoly. I would have thought that rating would be higher because (a) most parents don't know what's going on in their children's schools; (b) even more nonparents don't know what's going on in the schools; (c) some rural and suburban local school districts have not yet descended into the kind of moral insanity, social experimentation, and mind control into which larger urban districts have plummeted; and (d) so many have bought into the lie that the only real problem with public education in this country is that we're not spending enough money on it. Nevertheless, despite all those factors, two-thirds of the population is skeptical—perhaps even cynical—about their local public schools.

About 46 percent say they trust the neighborhood in which they live. That sounds about right. If half the people in this country live in nice neighborhoods, it makes sense that the other half wouldn't trust their not-so-nice neighborhoods. About the same number trust their local police departments. A slightly higher amount, 51 percent, actually trust their bosses. That's nice, given how much more contact people have with their supervisors at work than they do with their police departments—at least most people.

A much bigger group, 78 percent, trusts their local fire departments. Given the fact that in many communities in America the fire department is made up of volunteers, I guess that's understandable.

But look at this: 84 percent of people trust the members of their immediate families. Isn't that great? It would be awful not to trust your family members, but let's face it: There are a lot of creeps out there who are members of families. Still, people understand that this is the institution that has the best shot at solving problems—be they social, physical, emotional, or economic.

However, the institution that is taking over more and more responsibility for solving those problems—government—gets abysmally low marks from the overwhelming majority of Americans.

According to the poll, only 14 percent trust local government. Even fewer, 9 percent, trust state government. And only 6 percent of Americans have any faith in their federal government.

You have to ask yourself, Why are we giving the institutions that almost no one in the country trusts more and more power and authority in our lives? At the same time, why are we tearing asunder the one institution—the family—that seems to work?

The good news is that there is fertile ground for organizing if these statistics are even close to being true—and I suspect they are.

The trouble with Americans is not that they trust government in general. It is that they trust it specifically. Let me explain. Very few rational people really think government—especially big government—represents the most efficient way to solve problems. But Americans have become so conditioned by the media, their schools, and other cultural institutions to believe that government is the *only* legitimate way to solve problems. They no longer look to the family or the community to solve problems—even though they are institutions much more trusted than Washington. Instead, they trust government a little bit here and a little bit there, just in a few specific areas. When stitched together, these narrow interests overlap into a suffocating patchwork tyranny. So, while people may like government up close, looking at the whole mess they are often less impressed.

The fact that so few Americans really have any confidence in government in general, at the big-picture level, is a good thing. It tells me we have a chance to take America back—and soon.

Jefferson intuitively understood the danger we faced as Americans—how national priorities could easily shift, how the rule of law could be lost, and how easily man could be corrupted. That's what he was getting at when he called for a revolution every generation or so—to reverse the trend toward tyranny.

I think if you are honest with yourself and compare our situation in America today with what the colonists faced in 1776, you would have to agree with me that our freedom is more gravely threatened today than it was then.

Farah, how can you say that? you might wonder. *After all, at least we have our independence today. America is the greatest superpower in the whole world. Back then, America was battling the greatest superpower in the world.*

Precisely.

Today Americans are every bit the colonial people we were in 1776. A foreign power attempts to control every move we make—to regulate our actions with tens of thousands of arcane laws that can put anyone behind bars who steps out of line.

Think about it: "*colony* (1) a group of people who settle in a distant land but remain under the political jurisdiction of their native land; (2) a territory distant from the state having jurisdiction or control over it" (*Webster's New World*).

Aren't Americans, in a sense, all colonists of the great imperial throne in the District of Columbia? We all pay tribute to this empire. We are, in reality, little more than serfs doing the bidding of those in the federal corridors of power in Washington. We're taxed without real representation. We're forced to support a growing army of federal police in our communities. And we face a growing threat of disarmament—one of the great fears of the colonists who touched off the American Revolution at Lexington and Concord.

What we are witnessing, sadly, is the decline and fall of the American Empire. The sun sets on every empire established by man, and ours will be no exception.

One of the most popular books of all time is *The Decline and Fall of the Roman Empire*, written in 1788 by Edward Gibbon. The book set forth five basic reasons why great civilizations wither and die: (1) the undermining of the dignity and sanctity of the home, which is the basis for human society; (2) higher and higher taxes and the spending of public money for free bread and circuses for the populace; (3) the mad craze for pleasure—sports becoming every year more exciting, more brutal, more immoral; (4) the building of great armaments when the real enemy is within—the decay of individual responsibility; and (5) the decay of religion—with faith fading into mere form, losing touch with life, losing power to guide people.

The average age of the world's civilizations has been two hundred years. Civilizations and empires tend to progress through this sequence, say historians:

- from bondage to spiritual faith,
- from spiritual faith to great courage,
- from great courage to liberty,
- from liberty to abundance,
- from abundance to selfishness,
- from selfishness to complacency,
- from complacency to apathy,
- from apathy to dependence, and
- from dependence back again to bondage.

America is more than two centuries old. Where do you think we as a nation are in that sequence?

I've even stopped wishing my fellow Americans a "Happy Independence Day." Nothing would give me greater pleasure than to give such a greeting and mean it. But it would be disingenuous of me to do so. You see, I don't believe Americans any longer celebrate, cherish, or appreciate independence. Now we have lost our independence. And I'm not going to pretend otherwise.

Sadly, most Americans won't miss the greeting. They very likely don't even realize that Independence Day is the name of the holiday we celebrate on the Fourth of July in America.

It's not just the day we shoot off fireworks. It's not just the day we barbecue burgers. It's not just the day we go to the beach. It's Independence Day—so named because on or about this date in 1776, a group of courageous men risked their lives, their fortunes, and their sacred honor for a dream of freedom and sweet autonomy from an imperial power.

It wasn't just the birth date of American freedom. It was the birth date of freedom around the world.

But independence is no longer considered an ideal. More often, today, we hear about how our world is "interdependent." This is considered a good thing. Keep in mind every time you hear that word glorified that interdependence is simply another form of dependence.

I write often about freedom, but have never defined it.

Freedom, in the classical liberal tradition, exists only within the context of three conditions: self-government, civil rights, and the rule of law. Take away any one of these prerequisites and you seriously erode a nation's claim to freedom.

When less than 50 percent of the eligible public chooses to participate in a presidential election and there is widespread disenchantment with both major political parties, the system of self-government is clearly in danger.

When new "special" rights are bestowed upon favored classes of people because of their race, gender, or behavior patterns, the universal rights that transcend government edict are cheapened and assaulted.

And most of all, when the rule of law no longer applies to those in the most powerful positions of authority, the system is headed for a breakdown. It is the undermining of this last prerequisite of freedom in America today that threatens to knock the country off its enviable pedestal of liberty.

Let me give you an example or two of what I'm talking about. In 1993, incoming President Bill Clinton fired every single U.S. attorney in the country and replaced them with his handpicked choices. At the time, some Clinton critics postulated that this action was designed to camouflage the derailing of investigations into financial scandals in Arkansas. While indeed that may have been a consideration, with the benefit of hindsight we should be able to see the action laid the groundwork for much more unaccountable behavior over the next eight years.

This was a move designed to remove what Vice President Al Gore, later caught red-handed illicitly using his high office for overtly political purposes, would call the "controlling legal authority." It was the first of many programs designed to place the administration above the law. It was the beginning of an effort to remove any legal accountability of a future pattern of criminal activity. It was the end of responsibility to anything but public-opinion polls.

With just that one nearly unnoticed political move, along with the summary firing of FBI Director William Sessions in the administration's first year in power, Clinton cleared the field for a broad pattern of abuse of power—misusing the White House Travel Office, misusing the confidential FBI files of political adversaries, misusing the Internal Revenue Service to target enemies and stifle opposition, misusing other federal law enforcement agencies to cover up crimes, misusing federal employees to conduct purely political work and damage-control operations, misusing the office of the presidency to sell favors to private interests, including hostile foreign powers, and, yes, even misusing White House interns and volunteers.

If only Nixon had been this clever—if only he had planned ahead for the criminal activity in which he would participate—he would have served out his two terms in office. Nixon, however, waited until he got into trouble before he started firing the controlling legal authorities. Clinton removed them in advance.

That's how fragile the rule of law is in America. Dramatic actions are taking place right out in plain sight by the highest officials in the land, and Americans are generally oblivious to them.

This is how the end could begin for two hundred–plus years of increasing freedom in America. The attacks on liberty come from the top. They always do. Power is the enemy of freedom—the polar opposite. And what we see developing in Washington today is a centralization and consolidation of raw, unprincipled, unaccountable political power.

America has forgotten the two concepts that made her special as a nation—two unique factors that set her apart from the world from the start.

First, the founders wrote a Constitution that strictly limited the role of the federal government in the lives of Americans. The idea that Washington had some role in education, redistribution of wealth, setting minimum wage requirements, nationalizing millions of acres of land, taxing income, and subsidizing government-approved artists would have been anathema to the men who fought so valiantly for freedom against an overreaching foreign tyranny.

Second, the framers of that Constitution spoke eloquently about the fact that only a moral people—a nation of godly people with common spiritual and social values—were capable of self-government. They could not have envisioned the depths of depravity, licentiousness, and vice to which our society has fallen—though they warned about it.

Our current debates about social and government policy seem disconnected from these two critical foundations of the American republic. Politicians will never solve the problems facing the country without acknowledging these two essential precepts. In fact, the more government tries to do, the worse things get.

It's time for a radical new agenda—a Second American Revolution—to move the nation away from the idea that the federal government represents some large feeding trough through which we can all better ourselves materially. The only way Americans can reestablish their freedom, their God-given rights to life, liberty, and the pursuit of happiness, is to break the hammerlock of statism and the notion that morally relativistic secular humanism holds the answers to controlling men's passions and behavior.

Have you heard even one proposal come from Washington that held the promise of moving America in such a bold, new direction? It sure wasn't 1994's short-lived "Contract with America." It's time to return to the principles that made America the greatest experiment in self-government in the history of the world. It's time for a "Contract with the Constitution."

I am not a politician or a policy wonk. Nor am I vain enough to suppose I could come up with an entire agenda for redirecting the course of a nation. But someone, somewhere, somehow, has to start raising the real issues that must be addressed if America is to survive, let alone prosper, in the twenty-first century. So here are some of my suggestions right now:

- Abolish the income tax and the Internal Revenue Service.
- Withdraw from the United Nations, the World Trade Organization, and other globalist traps, and reaffirm America's commitment to sovereignty and self-government.
- Repeal the minimum wage and reestablish the right of individuals to freely enter commercial and employment agreements without interference from Washington.
- Eliminate all foreign aid.
- Abolish the departments of Education, Health and Human Services, Housing, Commerce, Veterans Affairs, and Agriculture.
- Eliminate the National Endowment for the Arts, the Corporation for Public Broadcasting, and the Federal Communication Commission.
- Abolish the Environmental Protection Agency, the Bureau of Land Management, U.S. Fish and Wildlife, and the Federal Emergency Management Administration.
- Privatize all federal lands.
- Privatize Social Security.
- Privatize Medicare.
- Abolish the Bureau of Alcohol, Tobacco, and Firearms.
- Repeal all national gun laws.

- Eliminate all subsidies—direct or indirect—to individuals or corporations.
- Repeal the War Powers Act and reestablish Congress's authority to declare war.
- End limits on federal campaign spending, enforce bans on foreign contributions, and require full disclosure of political contributions on the Internet.
- Repeal all presidential directives and executive orders.
- End all federal disaster relief without an act of Congress.

Feel free to add to the list. This is a revolution in the making. Let's start thinking of this agenda as a "living document" and stop thinking of our Constitution that way.

Furthermore, let's remember that these are merely political ideas and wholly inadequate to address the perilous moral and spiritual decline in which America finds itself. Don't expect politicians—especially the current crop in Washington—to provide any guidance or leadership of this kind. For that we should look to our churches and synagogues. We must insist that our spiritual leaders stand up, speak out, and be counted, just as we require our politicians to do so.

And most of all we must pray: Pray for the future of America. Give thanks to God for the blessings He has bestowed on this great nation in the past and rededicate ourselves to providing our children the opportunity for moral self-government. Pray for His help in taking America back.

$\star$ **3** $\star$

WHATEVER HAPPENED TO THE CONSTITUTION?

[T]here is no form of government but what may be a blessing to the people if well administered; and I believe, further, that this [the Constitution] is likely to be well administered for a course of years, and can only end in despotism, as other forms have done before it, when the people shall become so corrupted as to need despotic government, being incapable of any other.

—BENJAMIN FRANKLIN

ON SEPTEMBER 17, 1787, THE CONSTITUTIONAL Convention, having met in Philadelphia for four months, agreed on the final draft of a special, inspired document and submitted it to the several states for ratification. It was ratified on June 21, 1788, when New Hampshire approved it as the ninth state. Congress, acting under the Articles of Confederation, declared the United States Constitution the law of the land on March 4, 1789.

By general assent and resolution of the Congress, September 17 has thus been designated as Constitution Day ever since—designated, but not necessarily acknowledged or observed.

We celebrate many holidays in America today—Independence Day, presidential birthdays, Veterans Day, Memorial Day—yet no one even

37

acknowledges Constitution Day anymore. That's tragic. And it's symptomatic of a larger problem—the total disregard of this unique document in our public life.

As pointed out in Chapter 2, America has forgotten the two key concepts that made her unique as a nation: a constitutional commitment to limited government and a strong moral core that advanced self-government over statist government.

Hence the inherent beauty of the Constitution. It strictly limits what government can do. Unfortunately, Americans have forgotten this. They've been dumbed down by government schools and a government-media complex to believe that Uncle Sam is there to solve all their problems—from how much they get paid to what they spend on health care to how they should raise their own children.

We honor the flag in America, but not the Constitution. The flag is a mere symbol. The Constitution is the real thing. We should revere it, and more important, live under it.

While the Constitution is the real thing, it is also every bit as symbolic as the flag. It is literally a guidepost to maintaining—or now, perhaps, to recovering—America's freedom. But it can only serve that function if we as a nation abide by it, pay heed to it, live by its code and its spirit. We need to honor it. We need to understand it. We need to hold politicians accountable to it.

It's tragically ironic that we have millions of Americans who are perfectly willing to die for the flag of the United States yet are just not willing to live under the Constitution.

Which symbol is more important to us? The flag is not my pick. After all, it is *just* a symbol. Symbols, of course, are important. But the Constitution is more. It is both symbol and substance. And its substance is being desecrated by some of those who are so piously concerned about the symbolic desecration of the flag.

In July 2000, WorldNetDaily.com (WND) reported on a Portrait of America survey that found that less than half of American adults would vote for the Constitution if it were on the ballot today. To that

I say, "Thank God there is no requirement for a referendum on the Constitution."

One month later, WND reported on a poll that showed close to half of Americans don't believe in the basic First Amendment guarantees of freedom of speech, assembly, religion, and the press. To that I say, "Good riddance." Let those people find their own country. Make them get out. The Constitution is not for sale. It's not up for a vote. It's not a popularity contest. It's the law of the land. Love it or leave it.

It's time for real Americans—people who believe in this country—to take a stand. It's time to stop being wishy-washy about our principles. It's time to stop tolerating people who seek—knowingly or unknowingly—to subvert our heritage of freedom. America is *not* a democracy. I know you hear that it is in government schools. I know you hear that it is in the establishment press. I know you hear that it is from politicians.

Americans have become conditioned to believe we live in a democracy and that democracy is wonderful. Not only is democracy not wonderful, but America is *not* one, and never has been. And God willing, it never will be.

This is no small point. This is not a technicality. It's an important issue to understand. Democracy is always a disaster. The founders of this once-great nation understood that.

On September 18, 1787, after Benjamin Franklin signed the Constitution in Philadelphia, a woman reportedly asked him, "Well, Doctor, what have we got, a republic or a monarchy?" Franklin's answer: "A republic, if you can keep it."

Whether or not we can keep it is still an open question. But we have no chance to maintain a free republic—or to reestablish one in this country—if we the people do not even understand the objective.

Democracy destroys freedom. It always has, and it always will. It was the death knell of Athens, as Plato himself noted in *The Republic*. "Democracy," he said, "passes into despotism." The philosopher called democracy "a charming form of government, full of variety and disorder, and dispensing a sort of equality to equals and unequals alike. We know her well . . . In what manner does tyranny arise?—that it has democratic origins is evident . . . And does not tyranny spring from democracy in the same manner as democracy from oligarchy?"

While our Constitution, Declaration of Independence, and other founding documents never mention the word *democracy,* there is a popular misconception today that we live in one. And that misperception—that ignorance—is as dangerous to the health of our republic as it would be if our founders had made the tragic mistake of creating a democracy.

Democracy is little more than mob rule—dictatorship by majority opinion. It almost always ends in oppression of minorities—be they religious, ethnic, racial, or political minorities. Rule of law beats rule of mob any day. It is one of the reasons the American War for Independence was such a blessing to humanity and why the French Revolution was, in many ways, such a curse.

Majority rule was never the intent of our founders. They believed in the rule of law, not the rule of men. They understood that because of the fallen state of man, he would inevitably vote himself into slavery and tyranny if provided the tools.

Instead, as Franklin points out, America was created as a representative constitutional republic—one with checks and balances built in, with a Constitution, with a federal government of limited power and scope, a system in which the individual's inalienable rights were recognized and protected, a representative form of government, not one based on direct vote of the populace. And thank God for that.

Why don't democracies work? Because they are merely temporary states—transitional forms of government. They can only function until a majority of voters discover they can vote themselves money and other goodies from the public treasury. At that point the majority votes for candidates who promise the most benefits to them and the economy collapses because of increased taxation and spending.

That pattern is always followed by dictatorship. Always.

What is the difference between a democracy and a republic?

In a democracy, the majority can pretty much do whatever it wants. It can change laws, it can decide to oppress and exploit certain people. The ultimate authority is the will of the people—no matter how misguided and shortsighted it might be. In a republic the rule is by law. There are limitations explicitly placed on what government can and cannot do—no matter how popular the decisions might be.

There is no question that America is moving rapidly toward the democratic model and away from the republican model. Let's face facts. The federal government in Washington no longer feels bound to the Constitution, nor to the limits explicitly placed on it.

This is why we are so close to tyranny and despotism. We've lost our bearings. We've forgotten our history. And thus, we are doomed to repeat the mistakes of the past.

The Constitution, along with the Declaration of Independence, represents more of a national creed and mission statement for our country than it does a simple founding document. But the nonbelievers are winning the day. Not even the Constitution—that brilliantly crafted, inspired document—has the power to hold us together today.

Maybe, instead of reciting the Pledge of Allegiance to the flag in school every day, that time could be better spent reading the Constitution. And maybe if, instead of saluting the flag, our elected representatives in statehouses across the country and in Congress spent their time studying the founding documents—and reaffirming their oaths to them—our country would be a lot better off.

When did America lose sight of its constitutional heritage? There are many points in U.S. history at which radical shifts in thinking and policy occurred. Surely the War Between the States represents one such radical shift. The federal government usurped powers from the states before, during, and after that conflict.

Likewise, in 1913, another radical shift took place. That was the year the federal income tax was instituted. More on that later. But few Americans realize how radically America was changed in 1913 with the passage of the Federal Reserve Act.

Maybe most Americans don't even care.

How does the Federal Reserve Board affect my life? they think. *What do I know from Alan Greenspan? He's the guy who decides what interest rates are, right?*

The truth is the Federal Reserve, created in 1913, is a wholly unaccountable, private institution that affects the life of every American—probably more directly and profoundly than does the president of the United States. That's why Greenspan is often referred to as the most powerful man in America.

The Federal Reserve Act of 1913 was an attempt to take advantage of popular opinion in the United States for banking reforms. In effect, however, it was not reform at all. It was a power transfer—a coup in which a small group of bankers got a blank check to set monetary policy—and thus, all policy—for the entire nation. No watchdogs. No guardrails. No accountability. Zilch.

The very name *Federal Reserve Bank* was designed to deceive. It is not federal. It is not a government agency. It is privately owned. In short, it is nothing more than a group of private banks charging interest on money that never actually existed.

"Oh, Farah," you're probably saying right now, "whoa, fella. This is too much for me to absorb. Are you sure about this? This sounds like conspiracy stuff. Why isn't anyone talking about something so amazing?"

In a nutshell, here's how this Fed scheme works: The government prints $100 billion in interest-bearing U.S. bonds and takes them to the Federal Reserve. The Federal Reserve places the $100 billion in a checking account and the government writes checks against the balance.

In other words, we—the American people—allow this private banking system to create money out of thin air. And the bankers get interest on it—forever.

It's a legalized counterfeiting operation—pure and simple.

Way back in 1931, Louis T. McFadden, chairman of the House Banking and Currency Committee, saw the problem: "The Federal Reserve Board and banks are the duly appointed agents of the foreign central banks of issue and they are more concerned with their foreign customer than they are with the people of the United States. The only thing that is American about the Federal Reserve Board and banks is the money they use."

"Mr. Chairman," he pleaded on the House floor a year later, "we have in this country one of the most corrupt institutions the world has ever known. I refer to the Federal Reserve Board and the Federal Reserve Banks . . . Some people think that the Federal Reserve Banks are United States government institutions. They are not government institutions. They are private credit monopolies which prey upon the people of the United States for the benefit of themselves and their foreign customers; foreign and domestic speculators and swindlers; and rich and predatory money lenders. In that dark crew of financial pirates there are those who would cut a man's throat to get a dollar out of his pocket; there are those who send money into the states to buy votes to control our legislation; and there are those who maintain an international propaganda for the purpose of deceiving us and wheedling us into granting of new concessions which will permit them to cover up their past misdeeds and set again in motion their gigantic train of crime."

What does the Federal Reserve Board have to do with the U.S. Constitution? Nothing. That's why Congress had no authority to approve the Federal Reserve Act in 1913.

But that's just the tip of the iceberg in regard to the way Congress, the president, and the Supreme Court ignore the Constitution on a daily basis. All three branches of our government are in contempt of the Constitution.

We have entire bureaucracies established now—costing tens of billions of dollars—that have no justification for existence under the Constitution. That bothers me. How about you?

Worse yet, this culture of intrusive, busybody government, bred in Washington, is rapidly spreading across America. This mind-set suggests that elected and nonelected officials somehow have power over individuals' rights to life, liberty, and the pursuit of happiness.

Imagine the home you own and dream of someday handing down to your children and grandchildren—a home with memories money can never buy—is threatened with seizure by the government. Why? Because the government thinks your real estate and the property owned by your neighbors would be better used as the site of a new shopping center—one that can bring more tax revenue into the city's coffers. Your compensation is set unilaterally by the government entity that insists your home is just not in the "community's best interest." Sometimes there's a little payola involved too.

That is happening today more than you realize—unless you yourself have been victimized by this "eminent domain" mania. If your neighbor isn't safe from such exploitation by government, you aren't either. Nobody is.

Government at every level is corrupt—drunk with power. I feel it myself on a day-to-day basis as I drive roadways patrolled with eager-beaver patrolmen hoping to catch me and other unsuspecting motorists in speed traps. The more tickets, the more revenue. No warnings anymore. Warnings don't bring in revenue. Now many local police are handing out fines for not wearing seat belts too.

Think about the crazy asset-forfeiture laws being drafted in all fifty states and in Washington. They allow your car, your home, and your property to be seized because police say drugs were found. No trial is necessary. No offense needs to be proved in a court of law. The word of a cop is all it takes for you to lose your life savings—even if you had nothing to do with the supposed offense.

Now federal plans are under way to turn one of every twenty-four Americans into a domestic spy—a snitch who will rat on his neighbors if he suspects them of any antigovernment or subversive activity. That percentage of informants is higher than the one used by the dreaded East German Stazi secret police at the height of its Stalinist power. Under the plan, as first exposed by reporter Ritt Goldstein in the July 15, 2002, *Sydney Morning Herald,* your mailman, your utility meter reader, or the local train conductor could all be government snoops. They will help the government maintain dossiers on you—secret files that will be kept from you so that you can never challenge the authenticity or accuracy of the information gathered.

What country is this, anyway? Whom is the government supposed to be representing?

In America we're supposed to have a government of the people, by the people, and for the people. Even more important than that is that we are supposed to live under the rule of law. Thus, property owners ought to be secure in the knowledge that, barring extreme circumstances that might pose severe hazards to their neighbors, they will be able to use their property and develop it as they see fit.

That is no longer the case. And Washington is only the worst of the government culprits encroaching on property rights.

Property rights are fundamental. They are literally the building block of a free society. Without them, none of our freedoms amount to a hill of beans.

What all of these abuses have in common is that government is making decisions based on its own economic interests—not yours, not the interests of citizens, not the Constitution, not the rule of law.

When it comes to property rights, there are no absolutes anymore in America. And if property rights are not absolute, then no rights are.

Some people in America place a higher value on free-speech rights than rights to property. Yet, free-speech rights are derived from the concept of property rights. The founders believed that ideas were akin to property—and that's why they safeguarded speech and freedom of religion in the First Amendment.

It's time for citizens to say, "We've had enough!" America is supposed to be a land of limited government—of self-government— where responsible people are expected to make responsible decisions based on their self-interest.

Grown-up, sovereign individuals do not need nannies—especially nannies who impose their wills at the point of a gun. We don't need secret police monitoring our every activity. And we sure don't need to be numbered.

I have in my possession my original Social Security card, issued in the late 1950s. My mother got it for me when I was a small child. She did what she was told by her government. She believed in the authorities who told her, in writing, that the number would be used for Social Security and tax purposes only and "not for identification," as it clearly states on the card.

But my mother was betrayed by her government. That number has followed me like an albatross around my neck for the last forty years. I can't open a bank account without it. I can't get a driver's license without it. I can't even get a job without it. (I couldn't even get a contract to write this book without it.)

I don't want my kids to face that kind of future, nor, more likely, one much worse. I don't want my kids numbered by the government. I don't want to go along and get along with the king—for deeply held spiritual and philosophical reasons.

Yet because of this decision not to number my children, I pay significantly higher taxes than my neighbors who are given deductions because of their submission to the numbering system. My kids will not be permitted to work unless this abominable system is changed. They will no doubt face challenges in college admissions and in other areas.

That's why I am calling for an end to this numbering fascism. I want you to stand up and join me. We need a rebellion against invasions of privacy. Americans should be able to conduct business with each other without the government butting in and getting involved in the simplest and most innocent transactions. That's what freedom is. We don't have it when the government monitors everything. It's time to reclaim our God-given individual rights.

The Bible makes clear that numbering the population is God's jurisdiction and His only. He ordered Moses to do it (Num. 1). The Jews were blessed for it. But He did not order David to do it. Therefore David and all of Israel were punished for the king's misuse of authority (2 Sam. 24).

I for one will no longer voluntarily yield to illegitimate government authority—not on this. But more people need to say no. That's the way change occurs. That's the way freedom is restored. That's the way revolutions are fought. I hope and pray there are millions of other like-minded Americans out there who will begin standing up for God, country, Constitution, and individual liberty in this way.

Jesus said to render unto Caesar the things that are Caesar's and render unto God the things that are God's. God is the One who reserves the authority to number us. He even numbers the hairs on our heads.

It's time for Caesar to figure out some other system of getting his share.

I suspect one technique the government will use to get its share is brute force. According to the U.S. Justice Department, there are nearly a hundred thousand armed federal law-enforcement officers in the country. That statistic was released well before September 11, 2001, and there are now plans for a massive buildup of those law-enforcement resources.

You might think most of those would be in agencies with familiar initials—the FBI, DEA (Drug Enforcement Administration), INS (Immigration and Naturalization Service), or the U.S. Marshals Service. If so, you'd be wrong. Only thirty-three thousand of that total figure into the ranks of those agencies.

Since Bill Clinton took power in 1993, the number of federal cops has risen steadily. Back then, there was a total of sixty-nine thousand federal law-enforcement officers. What we've witnessed is the biggest arms buildup in the history of the federal government—and it's not taking place in the Defense Department. No, the kind of arms that are proliferating in Washington these days are the kind pointed at our own civilian population and carried by a growing number of federal police forces with ever-larger budgets and ever-deadlier arsenals.

But if most of the growth is taking place outside of traditional law-enforcement agencies such as the FBI, who's carrying the other guns? The answer is, simply, everyone from the postman to the Environmental Protection Agency field worker to agents of the U.S. Fish and Wildlife Service and the Army Corps of Engineers.

The arms proliferation at the federal government level is no joke. People are dying because of it—innocent people. Constitutional rights are being violated.

The founders of this country never envisioned the need for a federal police force. They saw the inherent dangers in such ideas. What we have today is a virtual standing army of armed federal cops.

Three disturbing trends are occurring all at once:

- Domestic police forces are being federalized, with state and local police increasingly coming under the authority and influence of Washington.

- The federal government and its law enforcement agencies are becoming increasingly militarized.

- The civilian population is being disarmed by new laws at the local, state, and federal level.

Perhaps it *is* time for gun control. Let's start by disarming the rogue federal cops. There's no authority for them in the U.S. Constitution, while the Second Amendment clearly safeguards the right of individual Americans to bear arms.

What hope is there to wake up Americans to all these threats to their liberties? There is some encouraging news. That same public-opinion survey that suggested Americans would vote down their own Constitution if they had a chance provided more information about what's really bugging our citizens. As pollster Scott Rasmussen explained in WND:

> The lack of support for the Constitution probably stems from the high levels of public disgust with government and politics today. Recent surveys have found that 72 percent of Americans now view the federal government as a special interest group that looks out primarily for its own interests. Only one out of four Americans believe their own representative in Congress is the best person for the job. Less than 40 percent think the government today reflects the will of the people.

Well, all that's encouraging, of course, because those people are exactly right. Except distrust of government should only lead people to believe more in the Constitution, not less.

Is there time to change course? Do Americans have the will to throw off the shackles to which they have so willingly submitted? Do we have the courage to recognize our errors and address them?

Yes, there's time—but it's getting late. Yes, some Americans have the will—perhaps just a tiny remnant. Yes, I have met many Americans who have the courage of their convictions and can and will do what is necessary to restore our freedom. That's why I wrote this book—to rally the remnant, to take America back. Are you still with me?

★ 4 ★

WHY YOU CAN'T TRUST GOVERNMENT

If in the opinion of the people the distribution or modification of the constitutional powers be in any particular wrong, let it be corrected by an amendment in the way which the Constitution designates. But let there be no change by usurpation; for though this, in one instance, may be the instrument of good, it is the customary weapon by which free governments are destroyed.

—GEORGE WASHINGTON

MOST AMERICANS THINK THEY ELECT MEMBERS OF CONGRESS to set priorities for national policy based on the Constitution, common sense, and a thorough examination of complex facts and circumstances the average citizen would never have time to consider.

The reality is that most members of the House of Representatives and Senate never even *read* the thousands of bills they vote to enact each year—let alone those they do not approve.

Did you catch that? They don't even *read* the bills!

That's the dirty little secret of Washington. How could our elected officials possibly evaluate the constitutionality of the legislation they approve, the rightness and wrongness of it, the actual impact it has on citizens, the fairness of it, the unintended consequences, and the cost and the extent to which it restricts freedom, without *reading* it?

Simple. They rely on staff reports, summaries, and recommendations. But no member's staff could ever read all the bills either. So they rely on two things to make their decisions: the recommendations of those sponsoring and supporting legislation and the recommendations of those opposing it.

Those two opposing forces often have strikingly different interpretations of what legislation means—not to mention how it will be uniformly enforced on a hapless citizenry.

That's why those who understand the process say, "There are two things you don't want to witness—the making of sausage and the making of law."

What Americans really need to understand is that every law passed by Congress is another restriction on your personal freedom. It's true in every case. Whether it is a law criminalizing an act heretofore considered legal or legislation requiring you to pay more of your money for some new responsibility of government. When Congress acts, freedom diminishes.

Our founders had a much different idea of the way things would work. They envisioned a government of citizen-legislators—part-time lawmakers who would spend a few weeks in Washington doing the business of the people and return home to tend the farm, run the ranch, practice law, or take care of other personal business.

There was no reason for full-time legislators, and plenty of reason to avoid them.

Nevertheless, two hundred–plus years later, America has a very full-time bicameral legislature—at least in terms of what taxpayers support. The approximately $150,000 each member of Congress earns hardly even begins to give you a full compensation picture. According to the National Taxpayers Union, members become eligible for pension benefits two or three times more generous than those offered in private business for executives in a similar salary range. These pensions are safeguarded against inflation, a feature fewer than one in ten private plans offer. Then there are the health- and life-insurance plans, the limousines, the prized parking spaces on Capitol Hill and at the two Washington airports, and travel expenses to home districts and other destinations.

But perhaps the greatest "gift" members of Congress give themselves at our expense is the across-the-board exemption from many tax, pension, and other laws they impose on us.

That's another dirty little secret of Washington. In other words, Congress frequently passes laws for ordinary peons like you and me with no intention of living under the consequences of those laws themselves.

A member of Congress who spends twenty to twenty-five years feeding at the trough of "public service" in Washington could collect $5 million or more in pension benefits. Compare that with the trifle you, the employer, get in Social Security benefits.

That's just some of what we pay to these able-bodied, and presumably able-minded, men and women—America's royalty.

For comparison purposes, what do we pay to the families—the widows and children—of true American heroes, men and women who give their lives in combat defending the nation? The direct death benefit is $6,000—and half of it is taxable.

Six thousand dollars! With all the money we spend on government and all the coddling we provide our elected elite, their priorities couldn't be screwier. And Americans sit by and watch in bemusement.

Compare that six thousand dollars paid to the widows and orphans of American military heroes with what U.S. taxpayers shelled out for the victims of the September 11 terrorist strike. Now, certainly this was a national tragedy unparalleled in American history. Yet I can't help asking myself these basic questions:

What constitutional rationale is there for direct payments to victims' families? If indeed there is a constitutional basis for some such payments, why not for others? Why not for the families of troops lost in Afghanistan? Why not for previous victims of al-Qaida terrorism at the U.S. embassies in Kenya and Tanzania and Khobar Towers and the USS *Cole*? Why not for victims of the previous World Trade Center bombing? Why not for the victims of the Oklahoma City bombing, TWA Flight 800—and on and on we go?

Yes, my heart goes out to the victims and their families. My prayers go out to them. Surely it is a noble endeavor to raise charitable contributions for the families. But taxpayer money? Why?

This is not compassion. This is coercion. And it points out a fundamental problem with the way Americans see their government.

Government is not Santa Claus. Government is government. It has clearly delineated powers and responsibilities—and clearly delineated areas of nonresponsibility.

Government is not supposed to make decisions from the heart. It is supposed to make decisions based on the will of the people—but only under the authority and scope of the Constitution.

There is nothing in the U.S. Constitution that would remotely authorize such a wealth transfer. Nothing.

Neither is there, of course, anything in the Constitution that would authorize Congress to give $15 billion to the U.S. airlines industry as a bailout after September 11—and this may be the inexcusable political motivation for the payments to the families. So often we see one bad government program lead to another. And that's what is happening here.

Yes, everyone feels awful about the losses these families experienced on September 11, 2001. So, few will raise their voices in protest. But it reminds me of the old Davy Crockett story, "Not Yours to Give."

Crockett eloquently explained to his fellow congressmen, intent on transferring federal funds to a widow, why it was not within their scope of responsibility and authority to do so. He offered, instead, real compassion—his own money.

That's the way it is supposed to work.

When government takes over the responsibility of charity, it undermines charity. It undermines our willingness—and ability—as a people to help our neighbors, our families, our friends.

Will future victims of terrorism also be treated this way? Government has now raised expectations.

Of course, there is precedent for giving money to victims of natural disasters. The misguided Federal Emergency Management Agency has carved out a special role for itself in giving away disaster aid for victims of severe floods, hurricanes, and storms. But this, too, is wrong. It's not only unconstitutional, it's unfair.

Why should those victims of large national disasters be compensated, but those anonymous victims of smaller, everyday tragedies go uncompensated?

Of course, some in our society might suggest that everyone be eligible for such compensation. There are always elements in our society who want to move America further down the road of socialism—a system in which government alone decides who gets what. Ultimately, it means none of us own anything. Our property is not our own. Government controls it all and decides how much, if any, you are allowed to keep, while redistributing the rest as it sees fit.

This victims' program, while certainly understandable in the wake of such a national tragedy, is hopelessly wrong.

Is there anything we can do about it? For those of us who understand just how misguided and immoral it is, we must speak out. We must not continue to make the same mistakes over and over. We must stop government from legalizing theft at every turn.

Want some examples of what your hard-earned tax dollars paid for in 2002? According to an April 15, 2002, report in *Insight:*

- $50,000 for a tattoo-removal program in California

- $450,000 to restore chimneys on Cumberland Island, Georgia

- $273,000 to help counter the influence of "Goth culture" in Missouri teens

Now, I don't like tattoos any better than the next guy. But whatever happened to personal responsibility? If people can afford to pay for tattoos that they later regret, shouldn't they be required to bear the consequences? I'm sure the chimneys on Cumberland Island are in a sad state of disrepair. But why should some working stiff three thousand miles away be forced to fix them? As far as the "Goth culture," I'd like to see the dark cult of piercing and uniformity eradicated, but aren't the folks promoting this pork-barrel spending the same people who are always preaching "multiculturalism" and "alternative lifestyles"?

An agency-by-agency inventory of government-owned cars found its fleet is bigger than the nation's leading car-rental company—more than 602,000 automobiles. That's a car for every three employees. According to an ABC News report, some agencies have more cars than employees.

It's not just money the government shells out that costs you, the taxpayer. Many of the laws passed by Congress cost you much more indirectly. As a June 2002 report by Citizens Against Government Waste points out, the cost of regulation drains the U.S. economy to the tune of $864 billion—yes, that's with a *B*—per year. That figure represents 8.4 percent of the nation's gross national product—the cost of every good and service throughout the economy.

With facts like these on the record, I'll never understand people—especially Americans—who think that government somehow has a monopoly on truth and justice. The more we rely on government to find truth and secure justice, the more we see how corrupt, how hopeless it is in doing either.

Take, for example, the government researchers who were caught planting false evidence of endangered species in national forests.

This outrageous and deliberate fraud against the American people by representatives of the government was discovered when a U.S. Forest Service employee blew the whistle on five U.S. Fish and Wildlife employees and two Washington state researchers who planted lynx hairs in areas where the cats did not exist. At your expense, the researchers were conducting a four-year study of fifty-seven forests in sixteen states to determine the extent of an endangered lynx habitat. But that's not what they were doing at all. This was not an objective, scientific study. It was an effort, on the taxpayers' dime, to create evidence to, pardon the expression, "buffalo" the taxpayer.

Had the fraud not been exposed—and you can imagine how many

similar ones are not—the findings of these rip-off artists would have been used to create sweeping new land restrictions against property owners, citizens who utilize the forests for recreation, and those who make their livings in the wilderness. Entire forests might have been shut down to the public, as they have been in many other locations across the United States—particularly in the West.

Again, it makes you wonder precisely how many times this has happened before.

The taxpayer-supported pseudo-researchers made their livings for four years deliberately bamboozling the American people.

How were they punished once they were caught? How did we make an example of them to discourage others from repeating this kind of fraud in the future? In which jailhouse are they residing now?

Are you sitting down?

The perpetrators of this fraud were not charged with any criminal wrongdoing. They were not fired from their jobs. They were not even disciplined, no punishment for the fraud whatsoever. They kept their jobs and were simply reassigned to other projects—where, presumably, their ecoactivism shrouded in the cloak of scientific research could be channeled into new efforts to shake down the taxpayer and maximize federal control of land and forests.

For my money, not only should the researchers have been fired and criminally prosecuted, heads should have rolled at all levels of the U.S. Fish and Wildlife Service—from the top to the bottom. This fraud calls into question everything this outfit has done or will ever do. All the research it has ever presented is now suspect. All the research it might do in the future isn't worth the recycled, biodegradable paper it is written upon.

The fraud also calls into question the fundamental principle of the Endangered Species Act. What is the purpose of this law? Is it really to protect wildlife? Or is there a bigger agenda?

It seems clear the actions of these government activists were motivated by something more than a desire to preserve cats in a natural habitat in which they did not reside. Clearly, it's about establishing more federal control over more land. That was the goal. It remains the goal. The charade has been exposed. Yet nothing is being done about it.

This fraud, by the way, was only discovered by chance by a dedicated and ethical Forest Service whistle-blower. But that agency, too, is responsible for more than its fair share of fraud and abuse.

While the lynx scam got more of the headlines, the Forest Service was forced to admit that it has lied to Congress and the public about the number of visitors to national forests. The agency claimed 920 million visitors in 2000, while the real number was 209 million.

Once again, the deceit was about money—bigger budgets, more control, larger bureaucracies, increased regulations, and more restrictions on access by the people who pay for it all.

So, please, don't tell me how we need the government to keep the private sector honest. We can always throw private rascals to the wolves when they violate the law. But the government rascals continue to get away with murder—and no one holds them accountable.

Do you want another example of how we're losing the very concept of private property at the hands of government-gone-wild?

Larry Halper is the last farmer in Piscataway, New Jersey, and he's learning that's not an enviable role. Halper grows pumpkins on a seventy-five-acre plot in the nation's most densely populated state. He's been offered, he says, up to $20 million by developers who would like to turn his little farm into an industrial park or a housing development.

He turned them down flat. He's a third-generation farmer, and he doesn't want to sell the farm out from under his seventy-nine-year-old mother and eighty-year-old aunt. You might think government officials, so concerned with preserving open spaces and greenbelts, would be pleased with his decision. They're not.

In fact, as the Associated Press reported, local officials are trying to force Halper, through eminent domain, to sell his land to them for less than a fifth of what private developers offered.

That's what the idea of "property rights" has come to mean in the twenty-first century. Your property really doesn't belong to you—it's more or less on loan from the government, which can call in that loan at its price anytime it pleases.

Let me tell you something, folks. If Larry Halper doesn't own his property and doesn't have the right to do with it as he pleases, none of us do. You don't have any rights over your home, your car, your children, or even your ideas. They are all just on loan from the government.

Larry Halper's plight is by no means an isolated one. He's facing the same predicament as thousands of others across the country who are coming to learn that "life, liberty, and pursuit of property" just doesn't mean the same thing it once meant in America.

Property rights shouldn't just be a concern of farmers and ranchers or big landowners out West. Property rights are the essential freedoms upon which all of our individual liberties are based. The founding fathers believed that freedom of speech and freedom of the press descended from the concept of property rights.

That's right. It is because we own our ideas and our consciences that we have the right to use them. The state no more controls our land—at least it's not supposed to—than it may control our thoughts. Once we as a people yield our God-given property rights to government, or accept that they are actually privileges and not birthrights, then we have not a leg to stand on in defending our free-speech rights.

While it's true we have a First Amendment that protects freedom of speech, freedom of the press, and freedom of religion from actions by Congress, we also have a Fourth Amendment, which protects people from unreasonable searches and seizures of their property. Yet those attacks continue—every day in America. How many laws do we have on the books in Washington today that infringe upon God-given inalienable rights? Nobody's even keeping track.

But it's hardly just Washington that is attacking property rights. The states are doing it. Local communities are doing it. And these attacks must be addressed by freedom-loving people before the masses accept the idea that government, at whatever level, is in control of everything.

Here's one more horror story for you—tragic but true. It illustrates how the forced redistribution of wealth by government, while sounding compassionate, brings out the absolute worst in people.

In Los Angeles, a medical clinic was found to be paying kids up to ten dollars to undergo unnecessary exams, including gynecological tests, and then billing the government. As reported in the *Los Angeles Times*, the LAPD says Paramount Medical Center employees picked up children between the ages of nine and fourteen from housing projects in south central Los Angeles, north Long Beach, and Compton in Southern California, and took them to the clinic. Each boy was reportedly paid five bucks. Girls got ten. Girls were paid more because gynecological exams could be performed on them, police said. The children were given prescriptions for spermicidal condoms and birth control following the examinations. Records and documents seized by police at the clinic indicate about a hundred boys and twenty-five girls were treated—or should we say, "mistreated"—every day.

And though the abuse of children is the most shocking and horrible aspect of this case, the practice wasn't limited to kids.

Jenaia Miller, twenty-five, says she made a regular practice of accepting the clinic's money. A van would pick her up and drive her from clinic to clinic, where she would undergo bogus examinations and be paid up to fifty dollars for six hours of "work."

It was easy money, she said. There was nothing to it.

And even though the scam was discovered when a parent of one of the children notified the police, not all parents saw it as a problem. Miller said parents often accompanied their children on these clinic visits.

This is the kind of corruption that you get when the natural controls of the free-enterprise system are removed and the government plays sugar daddy. This is why medical premiums are skyrocketing. This is why health-care costs are out of control. And, most important, this is why Americans today spend more on federal taxes than they do on housing, food, utilities, automobiles, and clothing—in short, all the necessities of life—combined. Did you realize that little factoid? This is compassion? This is fairness?

Most Americans don't even realize what they pay the government because the taxes are confiscated from them by their employers under penalty of law in the form of "withholding." That money is then sent directly to the government. Out of sight, out of mind.

The government creates problems, exacerbates them, and Americans plead for the government to solve them. This is the way politicians and bureaucrats empower themselves. There is no gutter too low for the government racketeers and their con artist collaborators to descend. They will molest your children, commit fraud, abort innocent life in the womb, sell drugs, and demand that you, the taxpayer, pick up the tab for all of it. When are we as a nation going to catch on?

This is business as usual in America today, folks. It's one big scam. It's organized crime, legalized theft. We only hear and read about the most extreme examples of it—and even then we don't hear or read much. The people who spoon-feed us the news are in on the racket. They're players. They love it. If they didn't, we would read stories about such abuse, waste, fraud, and corruption in government *each* day—in sources other than my own news agency, WorldNetDaily.com.

We don't. They're buried in the back pages of newspapers when they appear at all. Instead we read nonsense about the need to "save" Social Security, to "reform" welfare, to "reinvent" government.

I've got a better idea. Let's smash the feeding trough. Let's end welfare—not "as we know it," but as it really is. Let's not reinvent government; let's put it in its place, tame the monster, bring it under the control of the people and the Constitution, once again.

That's not likely to happen, however, until the people of south central Los Angeles, Compton, and north Long Beach realize who it is that's got that jackboot placed firmly on their necks. They don't even realize that they are living on the government's plantation. But it's not just them. It's all of us. We've allowed ourselves—all of us—to become slaves of the state.

We don't just need a tax revolt. We genuinely need a slave rebellion.

Too many Americans are ready to roll over anytime a government agency tells them to do so. They've become conditioned to believe that government is there to be their helper, their nanny, their parent.

Government, instead, my friends, is the gravest threat to your freedom. It always has been and it always will be. It's the only force on earth that can legally steal everything from you—your home, your property, your kids.

It's time to take government back—get it under control, force it to live under strict limits of authority and preserve freedom for future generations. It's time to take America back.

★ 5 ★

WHO'S GOING TO LEAD?

The time is now near at hand which must probably determine whether Americans are to be freemen or slaves; whether they are to have any property they can call their own . . . The fate of unborn millions will now depend, under God, on the courage and conduct of this army . . . Let us therefore rely on the goodness of the cause and the aid of the Supreme Being, in whose hands victory is, to animate and encourage us to great and noble actions.

—GEORGE WASHINGTON

AMERICA IS FACING A CRISIS OF LEADERSHIP.

In 1776, when America had a population representing only a tiny fraction of today's 300 million people, it was flush with brilliant and courageous leaders.

Think about it: George Washington, the indispensable military man and moral force; Thomas Jefferson, the inspirational writer and thinker; James Madison, the political genius; John Adams, the self-sacrificing diplomat; Benjamin Franklin, Samuel Adams, George Mason, Patrick Henry, and on and on. And Abigail Adams had more moxie than most of our male politicians today.

America was truly blessed with leadership.

Washington, D.C., is populated today by men and women who put their own careers ahead of national interest. Unlike the founders who risked everything—their lives, their fortunes, and their sacred honor—for freedom and independence, today's politicians are afraid even of being criticized.

They want to be loved. They want to be accepted. They don't want to be the bearers of bad news. And most of all, they don't want to be perceived as "intolerant." The very worst thing you can say about a politician, or someone else in public life today, is that he or she is "intolerant."

Let me tell you why I'm proud to be called "intolerant."

I'm intolerant of evil. That's a good thing. Tolerance of evil would be evil.

I'm intolerant of Americans who don't want to live within the confines of our constitutional system. That's also a good thing. Tolerance of unlawful behavior and the rule of men rather than the rule of law would be wrong.

I'm intolerant of ever-changing codes of morality. Another good thing. Tolerance of evolutionary morality is tolerance of amorality and immorality.

I'm intolerant of all these things—and I'm proud to admit it. And that's why I am intolerant of the political status quo in America today. I'm intolerant of the conventional wisdom of the day that suggests government has a solution for every problem under the sun. I'm intolerant of people who think they have a right to steal my property and redistribute it to their friends and constituents to buy political power.

I'm even more intolerant of politicians—elected leaders—who pledge to uphold the Constitution of the United States and knowingly cast votes in direct contradiction with that pledge. They should be imprisoned. Does that sound intolerant? Sue me.

While writing this book, I had the opportunity to attend a public policy luncheon in Washington where congressmen are called in for "off-the-record" briefings. Never again. I heard one official, one of the most "conservative" in the House, explain that he knew the entire Department of Education was unconstitutional, but what really upset him was that the president's education reform bill didn't include "school choice."

He might have voted for the bill and increased funding of the unconstitutional bureaucracy if only the president had thrown the conservatives this little, meaningless bone of "school choice." He also explained he would have to vote for the new "prescription drug" bill in the House because to vote against it would be political suicide.

I explained earlier in this book why I am not a conservative. But listening to rationalizations for unconstitutional behavior by congressmen really illustrated my gut feelings that "conservatives" will never win. They're not even trying to win—despite their occasional political rhetoric that might sound similar to mine.

They don't fight on offense. They are constantly in defensive posture.

Either we live by our principles or we don't have any principles. Conservatives today are letting liberals define them. They are defined by what they are against, more than what they are for.

I'm for constitutionally limited government. I'm for freedom. I'm for individual rights. I'm for self-government. I'm for personal responsibility and accountability to God.

The political status quo opposes all of that. That's why it's evil. That's why it must be destroyed. That's why we need to start over again with a clean slate. That's why we need a social and political revolution very much like the one that launched this great country in the eighteenth century.

We're not making progress. We're not expanding freedom. We're losing ground every passing moment.

Occasionally, the American people get a wake-up call and see this clearly for themselves. A good example came Wednesday, June 26, 2002. That was the date the Ninth U.S. Circuit Court of Appeals ruled it was unconstitutional for government schools to ask students to recite the Pledge of Allegiance.

The ruling stunned the nation. Radio talk-show hosts expressed outrage. A broad array of politicians denounced the decision. An avalanche of criticism prompted the judge responsible to place a stay on his own ruling.

Conservatives looked at the reaction to that ruling and saw something of a great political victory. Because of wide opposition, it seemed destined to be overturned. Maybe it will be.

But so what? What will be won if and when that decision is reversed? Will America be a better place, a freer place? Will the out-of-control judicial system responsible for the decision be reformed? Or will we have simply postponed the inevitable for another time?

I was not at all surprised by the ruling—and I really don't understand why any American would be. Sure it was wrong. Sure it had nothing to do with the Constitution. Sure it had nothing to do with common sense. But how much public policy in America today is right, constitutional, and derived of common sense?

Let's remember that in 1962 and 1963, the U.S. Supreme Court ruled that prayer in the schools was unconstitutional. The fact that it took nearly forty years for the other shoe to drop is something of a surprise to me.

You see, there are people in America—some of them in positions of significant power—who want to remake America in their own images.

The trouble is, America is the first country in the world to be created in the image of a godly nation. The founders studied the Bible to see what it revealed about the way men should govern themselves. There was never a thought in their minds about creating a country divorced from God and His laws.

Over the years, extreme secularists, materialists, socialists, and others have chipped away at the American creed—at the Constitution, at the Declaration of Independence. They have tried to convince us those documents don't really mean what they say. They have tried to persuade us that they are archaic and in need of updating. They have tried to explain that these statements are actually "living documents" subject to interpretation and reexamination under changing circumstances.

They have even tried to suggest that the gifted and inspired leaders who invented America, despite their words and deeds to the contrary, were not really Bible-believing Christians.

These activists have brought government into every aspect of our lives—despite specific constitutional prohibitions against overreaching federal power.

Now the architects of that unconstitutional way of life tell us we must conform to their ungodly standards. We must do nothing to offend them. We must not be "intolerant."

We can yell and scream about this all we want. But it won't change the direction of this country. What will? Ah, now we're getting to the real subject of this book—taking America back. There is a way, my friends. To get there, we need to be sure of ourselves, our beliefs, our principles, our purpose in life, our convictions—and we must always know that God is on His throne. He is in control of the universe. He empowers those who do His will, follow His laws, live for Him, honor Him.

The founding fathers were, almost all of them, sure about those things. They had courage. They knew what was right because they studied the Scriptures. They modeled their ideas of government on biblical precepts. They rejected ungodly government.

We must do the same. We need to stop fighting defensively. We need to get on the offensive—the only way, after all, you can ever score points. What do I mean? The conservative way to fight an unconstitutional ruling like the Ninth Circuit case would be to do one or all of the following things:

- work for a reversal of the ruling
- work for the impeachment of the judge
- work for new legislation specifically authorizing the reading of the Pledge in schools

Those may seem like good tactics. They may seem like the right thing to do. And there is nothing wrong with any of those ideas. The only problem is that, at best, they maintain the status quo—for the moment. If successful, they do nothing to address the real problem—unaccountable government, cultural suicide, the continued march toward immorality and relativism.

Victory in this case would be very fleeting indeed. The Marxist-Leninists of another generation understood what I am talking about. They had an expression—"two steps forward, one step back." Change, they knew, seldom came in dramatic style. It occurred gradually. And sometimes, for strategic reasons, it was worthwhile bending and yielding and allowing the other side to think it had achieved victory. That way they would be lulled into a false sense of complacency.

Another way to explain it is with the old frog-in-the-kettle analogy. I don't know if it's really true or not, but rumor has it that if you put a frog in a kettle and heat it slowly, the frog will relax and enjoy the increasing temperature. By the time it reaches the boiling point, it will be immobilized and unable to jump out of the pot. On the other hand, the story goes, if you heat the pot more quickly, the frog will be stunned by the rapidly increasing temperature and instinctively leap out to save itself.

Americans have been like that frog on a slow boil. We're conditioned to the slow degradation of our culture and political system. We're even comforted by the warmth it seems to generate with all of the seemingly lively debate. But the debate is an illusion. It's a deception. It only serves to disguise the fact that our goose is about to be cooked.

So how do we fight back effectively?

It's time for all of us who realize we're in hot water to jump out of the pot.

Take, for example, the Pledge flap. Spending our time and money fighting only to bring America back to the sad state of affairs that existed before the ruling is not a victory. What freedom-loving Americans should do in response to a decision like that is to call the bluff of those turning up the heat on us.

You see, I think the Pledge ruling is a good example of a strategic mistake by those cooking up a new world order for us. Someone turned the heat up too fast. They miscalculated. Instead of increasing the temperature by one degree, it went up ten. Too many people noticed the fluctuation. They were surprised. They were awakened from their hot-tub complacency. Some realized this wasn't a Jacuzzi they were in; it was a cauldron.

For those who want their country back—the America of self-reliance, of individual rights, of personal responsibility, of rule of law, of limited government—the Pledge flap represented a golden opportunity to call the bluff of those slowly but surely transforming our society into one our founders would scarcely recognize.

How do we do that? How do we jump out of the hot pot?

Whenever Americans are stunned and momentarily awakened from their slumber by a political miscalculation such as the Pledge ruling, we need to use the opportunity to rally them to revolt.

What form does that revolt take? If we're lucky and we act soon, we may be fortunate enough to avoid the kind of violent conflict our forefathers endured. Our revolution, with God's grace, might look more like the Second Russian Revolution in which few shots were fired. What the Russians did, you might recall, was simply say, "No."

That's what we need to say. For instance, the logical response to the Pledge ruling is to pull your poor children out of those government indoctrination centers known as schools. Every American outraged by the ruling should not even raise a whimper of protest. They should not argue. They should not complain. Instead, they should remove their children from these ungodly, hostile government schools. They should do it immediately. They shouldn't wait until the situation gets any worse.

The Pledge itself is not all that important, of course—not in the big scheme of things. There are much worse horrors taking place in government schools across America on a daily basis. Kids are taught techniques of aberrant sexual behavior. They are taught in a million ways that God is irrelevant to their education. They are taught pseudoscience cloaked in the "good citizenship" of environmentalism. They are intentionally denied the basic tools of self-government—

knowledge of history, geography, and good reading and learning habits.

All of this intentional programming has gone on for more than thirty years because it was imposed slowly—like the gradually increasing temperature on the frog's kettle. But the Pledge ruling gave the cooking frog a start. And we've got to use those opportunities when they arise to awaken the sleeping populace.

I don't know how many parents get it. I don't know just what percentage of the population it represents. I don't know how many millions of people are awakening like that frog in the pot. But I do know it is a very significant number—close to the critical mass needed to start successful revolutions.

What is that magic number? The Bolsheviks boasted of 3 percent. Three percent! Is there a 3 percent remnant in America today? I believe the number is considerably bigger than that.

In days gone by, we would have convinced each other that the way to respond to the problems we saw in American society was to "get involved." We would have persuaded our friends and family members and neighbors to vote, to join the PTA, to work on behalf of some politician, to give money to a political campaign.

The bad news is that those ideas don't work anymore. We're in such an advanced state of cultural and political decay that our efforts will only leave us disenchanted, discouraged, and demoralized. The good news is there's perhaps an easier way to achieve our objectives. We need to do what the Russians did when they ended seventy years of Soviet oppression. We need to just say no.

Saying no means pulling your kids out of those brainwashing hubs. Imagine what would happen if several hundred thousand parents did that this year—joining the growing millions who have already made that choice. Not only will you bring direct benefits to your kids—protecting them and providing them with the chance for a real education—but you will also be dropping out of the system, becoming part of the solution rather than part of the problem.

Homeschooling is the best option. For those who can't do that, choose a worthy private institution. It will be the best choice you ever made for your children. There are a thousand reasons for making this choice. The Pledge ruling just makes it a thousand and one.

I say let the atheists have the government schools. Let the homosexual activists have them. Let the socialists have them. Let them fight out the curriculum issues among their multicultural, tolerant friends. Jews and Christians should get out now.

What will they have? Not much. Meanwhile, your children might actually get educated.

If responsible Christian and Jewish parents did this all over America tomorrow, it would set off a revolution in this country. Gone would be the multibillion-dollar Department of Education boondoggle. Gone would be the condom education. Gone would be the sexual propaganda and the moral relativism. No way tens of millions of parents are going to continue to be soaked in taxes for schools they don't use. Not only will your children be liberated, the whole country would be.

That kind of revolution would spread. Freedom would soon be breaking out all over America.

The alternative is the kind of pathetic protest we have seen for years. If you act like a doormat for forty years, expect to be treated like one. If you invite abuse, expect it to continue. If you act like a slave, prepare to be treated like one.

This ruling may or may not stand the test of an appeal. That doesn't really matter. Either way, the schools are no longer your schools. You know that.

It's time for action, not words. It's time to be a part of the solution rather than part of the problem.

Just say no. Pull your children out.

This is the way parents should have responded forty years ago to the U.S. Supreme Court rulings. They should have picked up their kids and gone home. Instead they succumbed. They adapted to the changing morality; they did what they were told. It's time for new tactics.

Get your children out and don't look back.

Don't try to reform government schools. It can't be done. Let's shut them down. Let's turn them into museums of misguided ideologies. Let's turn them into bomb shelters or something else useful to society.

The time to act is now. There may not be too many more chances for freedom-loving Americans to respond, to take the initiative, to go on the offensive.

The cancer is spreading fast from Washington. For many years now, the federal government has been usurping the powers of the states. The federal court ruling on the flag salute is just one of thousands of examples.

Today, state governments mostly consider themselves subservient to the will of Washington—gladly accepting marching orders, pathetically holding out their hands for money extracted from their own taxpayers and generally serving as an extension of the federal bureaucracy.

It is only in that context that one can begin to comprehend the nightmarish, Orwellian nature of the latest federal-state power grab.

Let me illustrate the threat by telling you about the Model State Health Powers Act. Sounds innocuous, doesn't it?

Financed by the federal Centers for Disease Control, it was hatched in Washington with the cooperation of the National Governors Association, the National Conference of State Legislatures, the Association of State and Territorial Health Officials, the National Association of City and County Health Officials, and the National Association of Attorneys General.

What's so scary about the MSHPA?

It is a law being introduced in all fifty state legislatures, passing in many, that grants emergency powers to governors and public-health authorities—powers so sweeping they would make Benito Mussolini blush.

The act authorizes the collection of private medical data and other records on you and your family. It authorizes the "control of property"—a nice term for confiscation of everything, including—but not limited to—your house, your car, your guns, your food, your clothing, and your fuel. It authorizes the management of people—meaning forced vaccinations, incarceration, and restrictions on transportation. It also allows the government to seize control of communications.

Now, as I read that prescription, it smacks of tyranny. It reeks of fascism.

Under this model legislation, which is gaining steam across America, one man or woman—the governor—can declare a public-health emergency and assume all of the powers above.

Many believe that because this act came up after September 11, 2001, it has to do with bioterrorism or nuclear or chemical attacks. But the public-health emergency doesn't need to have any tie to terror.

This is serious stuff. It leaves me wondering if Americans are threatened more by terrorism or by the war on terrorism. Sometimes it appears our government no longer considers Osama bin Laden's ilk as public enemy number one. Now it's Joe Citizen who finds himself in the crosshairs. We're on the verge of losing our constitutional protections against illegal searches and seizures. We're being desensitized as a people every day.

Maybe you don't think your governor is a threat to your personal freedom. Perhaps you just think this is one more law that won't amount to a hill of beans or affect your life. Maybe you're right. Maybe. Then again, maybe not.

Remember, I told you that this legislation can only be understood in the context of the way Washington has the states under its thumb. Remember where this legislation originated. Remember who paid for it. Remember who is pushing it.

This debacle is evidence of a failure of leadership at the very top. Our government has steadfastly rejected commonsense antiterrorism measures, such as firearms in the cockpits, and instead favored building a command-and-control bureaucracy that will never make any of us safer.

It's easy being a civil libertarian when times are good—when there are no real threats on the horizon. The real challenge to constitutional government comes in times of crisis, in times of war, in times of attack.

There's no question we're in a real war against terrorism. But it's our own government, once again, that's really scaring me.

Aldous Huxley said it best half a century ago in *Brave New World Revisited*:

A really efficient totalitarian state would be one in which the all-powerful executive of political bosses and their army of managers control a population of slaves who do not have to be coerced, because they love their servitude. To make them love it is the task assigned, in present totalitarian states, to ministries of propaganda, newspaper editors and schoolteachers. But their methods are still crude and unscientific.

That was certainly true half a century ago. Today, I would suggest, the biggest change is that the methods are less crude, more scientific.

In fact, America is moving closer to totalitarianism and servitude—and most people don't even recognize it.

Who's going to lead us out of this morass? I've got a surprise for you. You are. Don't look to others. Don't look to your congressman. Don't look for some messianic new presidential candidate. Don't look to your favorite talk-show host. Don't even look to me—especially not me! Instead, look in the mirror.

How do we do it? No compromise. No retreat. No surrender.

We don't make peace with evil. We don't accept it. We don't live with it. We don't tolerate it. We resist it with all our might. If you begin doing that, and I begin doing that, and a few more people begin doing that, we just might be ready to take America back.

★ 6 ★

WHAT IS DEFENSE?

In the councils of government, we must guard against the acquisition of unwarranted influence, whether sought or unsought, by the military-industrial complex. The potential for the disastrous rise of misplaced power exists and will persist. We must never let the weight of this combination endanger our liberties or democratic processes. We should take nothing for granted. Only an alert and knowledgeable citizenry can compel the proper meshing of the huge industrial and military machinery of defense with our peaceful methods and goals, so that security and liberty may prosper together.

—DWIGHT D. EISENHOWER

AMERICA IS AT WAR AGAIN. THOUGH IT'S NOT A DECLARED war against a well-defined foreign enemy, we're told the conflict could rage for decades.

After September 11, 2001, there is little doubt Americans will experience this war here at home—not just as soldiers fighting abroad, but right here in our own homes, our own offices, our own streets, our own cities and towns. We're going to be among the casualties in this war—you, me, our children and grandchildren.

Despite spending billions and billions of dollars on "defense,"

Americans remain virtually defenseless against weapons of mass destruction wielded by terrorists and rogue nations hostile to the West.

There is a threat. It is considerable. The possibility of a nuclear attack, a biological attack, or a chemical attack on Washington, New York, or some other U.S. city is real. There are bad guys in this world. They are out to get us. They have real resources and real capabilities.

One man who gets paid to know about threats is Warren Buffett, the world's second-richest man, whose main business is insurance. Here's what he told investors on the final day of Berkshire Hathaway Inc.'s annual meeting on May 5, 2002: "We're going to have something in the way of a major nuclear event in this country. It will happen. Whether it will happen in ten years, or ten minutes, or fifty years . . . it's virtually a certainty."

Most Americans, most politicians, most pundits still don't get it. They don't comprehend that America truly is defenseless—despite all the billions of dollars we spend on "defense."

In America the very word *defense* has come to mean military spending. Just like in George Orwell's *1984,* the word has come to mean the opposite of what it really means. In the U.S. today, *defense* means "offense." It means projecting military power around the world. It does not mean defending American civilians.

Part of taking America back means redefining our terms, reestablishing sensible national priorities, reorienting ourselves to constitutional governance. No such reexamination would be complete without considering the way we think about "defense" today.

On September 11, 2001, foreign terrorists boarded four commercial airliners and crashed them. Symbolically, one of those planes crashed into the very heart of the U.S. defense establishment, the Pentagon.

It could have been much worse. And it will be someday unless Americans wake up to the fact that they have been left purposely defenseless by their government. Americans are perceived by their leaders as little more than collateral damage in the inevitable war of the future to be fought on our own homeland.

Let me be very clear: National defense is not about new weapons systems. It's not about new bombers. It's not about sophisticated new missiles. It's not about transport planes or battleships or carriers. It's not even just about some kind of impenetrable missile-defense system; even that wouldn't address all of the threats we as a nation face.

I'm talking about protecting you, your children, and your grandchildren from attacks that are coming as surely as you are reading this book today.

At this very moment, terrorists are planning to wreak havoc on America with weapons of mass destruction. Foreign rogue states are working on nuclear weapons technology with an eye toward achieving a kind of extortionist parity with the United States of America. Foreign nations you are supporting with your hard-earned tax dollars, and others your nation is propping up with preferential trade practices, have nuclear weapons pointed at America's cities—right now.

America is defenseless against all of these threats. Utterly defenseless—like some pitiful, helpless giant.

It would be a bad thing if our potential enemies were also defenseless, but they are not. They have used technologies developed here in the United States—technologies you, the taxpayer, have helped develop—and put them to use defending their people and infrastructure with an eye toward surviving a nuclear war.

In America we have convinced ourselves that nuclear war is not survivable—that it is not worth surviving. It's a defeatist mentality that ensures this country will not survive when the inevitable attack comes.

The Office of Homeland Security is *not* addressing this issue.

Let me ask you a few questions: If it makes sense to provide the federal government with bunkers and shelters, why doesn't it make sense to provide them for civilians? If they will serve the purpose of ensuring survival of the federal government, why won't they work to ensure that millions of Americans survive a cataclysmic attack? If civil defense makes sense for China and other countries that supposedly don't value human life as highly as we do in the West, why doesn't it make sense for us?

There is only one way to defend Americans from nuclear, biological, and chemical attack—to provide them with shelters.

It's not a new idea. It's an old idea. It works. It is feasible. It is not outrageously expensive, but it is vitally necessary. It should be the highest priority of the Defense Department. Yet it is not on anyone's radar screen.

President Bush has developed a "Continuity of Government Plan"—what some have called a "shadow government" that survives in the event of a devastating attack on Washington. Of course, that is an appropriate action in times like these. But now it's time to take the next logical step and create a "Continuity of America Plan."

This is a threat that won't go away if and when we ever capture or kill Osama bin Laden and the rest of his terrorist network. There will always be enemies like al-Qaida. There will always be external threats to our nation. There will always be the threat of nuclear detonations and weapons of mass destruction. There is no substitute for a shelter system. None.

How do we pay for it? Quite appropriately out of the Defense Department budget. That's what it's there for. Defense of the nation is the main reason we have a federal government under the Constitution. Protecting lives should be the first priority of the federal government. Ask yourself, instead, how and why we should pay for all the other nonsense Washington supports—with little, if any, constitutional authority. Why should we pay for protecting other countries' civilians and not our own? Why should we pay for sophisticated weapons of destruction and not for the simple tools of survival?

Today America deploys more U.S. forces to more foreign countries than ever before. Incredibly, at the same time, in the last decade we have witnessed U.S. military forces cut by 40 percent.

Consider a few facts: During the Eisenhower administration, the U.S. spent 16 percent of its gross domestic product on defense. Today, we spend 3 percent. Back then, the defense budget accounted for 62 percent of federal spending. Today, it's down to 15 percent.

From 1990 through the Clinton years, active Army ranks were reduced from 770,000 to 495,000. At the end of Clinton's term, the Army had ten active combat divisions compared to the eighteen it had at the start of Operation Desert Storm in 1991. What was cut? According to figures cited by pundit Mark Helprin:

- 293,000 reservists;
- 2 reserve divisions;
- 20 Air Force and Navy air wings with approximately 2,000 combat aircraft;
- 232 strategic bombers;
- 13 ballistic missile submarines with 3,114 nuclear warheads on 232 missiles;
- 500 ICBMs;
- 4 aircraft carriers;
- 121 surface combatants and attack submarines, plus all the support basing, transport and logistic access, tanks, armored fighting vehicles, helicopters, etc.

Despite the dwindling manpower and resources, during the Clinton administration, U.S. military forces have been asked to perform many more missions than they have in the past—most of them under the auspices of the United Nations and NATO. During 1997 alone, for instance, the First Armored Division was directed eighty-nine times to provide personnel for "peacekeeping" operations. The average soldier involved in such operations was deployed for 254 days out of the year.

The U.S. slashed the military budget every year since the Cold War ended with the idea that the major threat to American security has been eradicated. What most officials missed was the emergence of new and different threats—China, radical Islam, rogue terror states, and new nuclear powers.

Why don't Americans realize the extent of the threat—particularly the threat from weapons of mass destruction? Simple. Because they have been lied to by their government. Here's what Clinton said in his reelection effort:

February 16, 1996: "If you look at the role America has played in the world, we should be rejoicing . . . There are no more nuclear missiles pointed at any children in the United States. I'm proud of that . . ."

February 15, 1996: "I asked you to give me a chance to try to give America a more secure future and a more peaceful, more democratic world. And the fact that there are no nuclear missiles pointed at any American children for the first time since the dawn of the nuclear age is evidence of that commitment kept."

October 20, 1996: "There is not a single, solitary nuclear missile pointed at an American child tonight. Not one. Not one. Not a single one."

Over and over during his reelection campaign in 1996, President Clinton bragged about having ended the threat of nuclear arms to American soil—and, of course, to America's children. Those who bothered to inform themselves on such security issues understood that his boasts rang hollow—that Russian nuclear weapons could be retargeted on American cities in a matter of minutes. Nevertheless, few challenged the "technical" accuracy of Clinton's unambiguous claims.

It is impossible to know how critical to Clinton's reelection effort such phony claims were. But they were phony. There was nothing accurate about them at all. Not one thing. Not one. Not a single one.

In fact, according to the CIA, thirteen of China's eighteen long-range strategic missiles were aimed at U.S. cities. Clinton knew this. He lied audaciously and with a straight face to the American people about having ended the nuclear threat to our country's "children."

You might think, with a new administration in place and the war on terrorism under way, that there would be wide debate about such policies. You might also think there would be renewed discussion about civil defense. You might even think the defense of the American people might become a priority again. But the Bush administration has said and done little to suggest that a radical change in policy will be forthcoming.

We have hundreds of thousands of American service personnel stationed in more than 140 nations around the world. We have another

26,000 serving on naval vessels in foreign waters. Why? And when are we going to start bringing them home in droves?

Think about it. The U.S. still has 70,000 soldiers serving in Germany today. Germany! Those troops were deployed there during the Cold War, when the U.S. and western Europe feared a Soviet invasion was imminent. What is the rationale for keeping them there today?

The U.S. still has 40,570 troops in Japan. Are we worried the emperor is going to make a comeback and rebomb Pearl Harbor? Are we worried China is about to invade Japan? If so, why do we extend to China most-favored-nation trading status?

The U.S. still maintains 36,263 troops in South Korea. Now, this is one place where there is a constant threat of war. North Korea is still technically in a state of war with South Korea, and the U.S. may be able to justify the continued presence. But why isn't there any debate about it? Why aren't long-term alternatives to this policy being discussed? Are we going to defend South Korea forever? Wouldn't we be better off helping the South Koreans defend themselves against potential aggression?

The U.S. still has 11,564 troops occupying Italy. Why? Do we fear the reincarnation of Benito Mussolini? From whom are we protecting Italians? Themselves?

The U.S. even has 11,274 troops in Great Britain. Great Britain has a pretty good military force of its own. Don't we trust them to defend themselves?

The U.S. has a force of 7,169 in Bosnia-Herzegovina. What vital interests does the U.S. have there?

The U.S. maintains a force of 5,469 in Kuwait. Is Kuwait paying us for this protection? I don't think so. And the U.S. should not be in the mercenary business anyway. It's not in our Constitution.

The U.S. has 5,423 troops in Serbia, including Kosovo. Hey, Slobodan Milosevic is gone. He was arrested by his own countrymen. Enough is enough already.

There are 5,397 U.S. troops remaining in Saudi Arabia defending the wealthy tyrants in that desert country. Why should ordinary Americans pay with blood and hard-earned money to protect Saudi Arabia?

The U.S. has 2,123 troops in Spain; 2,105 in Turkey; 1,677 in Iceland; 1,598 in Belgium; 1,112 in Bahrain; 997 in Portugal; 774 in the U.S. Naval Base in Guantánamo Bay, Cuba; 670 in the Netherlands; 627 in Diego Garcia; and 517 in Greece.

There are smaller U.S. troop commitments in Kenya, Ethiopia, Yemen, Uganda, Russia, and twelve other countries that formerly comprised the Soviet Union.

Why aren't we talking about bringing any of these troops home? This would be a sensible way both to cut military spending and to get back to our constitutional republic. It would also be a sensible way to stop being the policeman of the world. And such cuts—these new priorities—would provide all the resources we as a nation would need to refocus our defense on protecting innocent Americans.

But no, there is no end in sight to this madness. We have not learned the lessons of every other empire in the history of the world that spread itself too thin, that overcommitted its resources, that didn't understand that every fight is not its fight.

Are there serious threats to American security in the world? You bet there are. But we can never be prepared for them with our military forces spread far and wide across the globe.

We're defending others, but not defending ourselves. Go figure.

Is there really a higher priority for the U.S. government than defending American citizens from an unprovoked nuclear, chemical, or biological attack? This is, after all, the principal responsibility of the federal government—not redistributing our wealth, not managing our property, not numbering us, monitoring our e-mail and our phone calls, not disarming law-abiding citizens, not even protecting us from discrimination. The Constitution charges the federal government, first and foremost, with the defense of our lives from foreign threat.

When that nuclear attack comes—and it will come—much of the government will be safely ensconced in bunkers outside Washington, D.C. Warren Buffett has probably built his own shelter. The rest of us will be on our own.

Let's characterize government's priorities for what they are—

selfishness. In every conceivable way, the federal government has for the last thirty years borrowed from our children and grandchildren to foster a greater sense of dependency among the people. It has interjected itself into every aspect of our private lives. No cost is too high when the government wants to indoctrinate your children, regulate your business, reward slothfulness, and score political points with the most unproductive sectors of the country.

But when it comes to defending Americans' lives, suddenly, the politicians grow cost conscious. Isn't it amazing? It's worse than that. It's treasonous. It's unconstitutional. It's immoral.

Most Americans, unfortunately, have no idea that they are completely defenseless when it comes to a nuclear attack. They have become comfortable. They evidently believe their government is actually working in their best interests. They believe antimissile treaties will protect them. And since they are already taxed at confiscatory rates, they eagerly accept the word of politically motivated generals who tell them it's just too expensive to protect them.

Washington needs to reassess its priorities. No more foreign aid. No more welfare. No more pencil pushers. No more intrusion into our lives. No more regulations. No more bureaucracies. No more federal cops. It's time to focus on the one clear-cut job the federal government has under the Constitution—defending the lives of Americans.

Now that America has been attacked by foreign enemies, now that we know our country is vulnerable, now that we understand there are still foreign terrorist moles operating inside the gates, it's time to encourage real Americans to defend themselves, prepare themselves. Here's some of what needs to be done:

- One efficient and commonsense way we can combat airline terrorism is to arm our pilots.

- It's time to ensure that every good American has access to firearms for the protection of family and community.

- Take the necessary precautions to protect Americans from radioactive fallout—the type that we can expect from a nuclear warhead or the kind of "dirty bomb" the terrorists have sought to develop.

- Secure our borders.

Most of all, however, Americans need to be enlisted in this war. They need to be empowered to defend themselves and their families. Americans have no idea what to expect or what is expected of them. Instead, they are being assured that everything that can be done is being done. It's not—and this is inevitably dangerous because, make no mistake about it, this is a real war.

Not a dime of your hard-earned tax dollars is actually being spent on protecting you, your children, your family, your neighborhood, or your town. That's what defense is all about. That's what Homeland Security really means. It means shelters from the inevitable attacks by nuclear, biological, and chemical weapons. It means antimissile batteries. It means stockpiling of food and medicine. It means radiation monitors. It means civilian evacuation drills. It means securing our borders from infiltration by potential terrorists. It means arming pilots and airline crews. It means arming Americans and encouraging them to be more self-reliant.

If we don't take these steps soon, there won't be an America to take back.

WHAT ARE WE PAYING FOR?

The income tax is fulfilling the Marxist prophecy that the surest way to destroy a capitalist society is by "steeply graduated" taxes on income and heavy levies upon the estates of people when they die.

—T. COLEMAN ANDREWS, FORMER IRS COMMISSIONER

And the tax collector, standing afar off, would not so much as raise his eyes to heaven, but beat his breast, saying, "God, be merciful to me a sinner!"

—LUKE 18:13 NKJV

LET ME REITERATE: AMERICANS TODAY PAY MORE IN TAXES than they pay for all other expenses *combined!*

Did you catch that the first time? If not, let me restate it: The average citizen pays more in taxes than for food, clothing, shelter, entertainment, transportation, and all other costs of living *combined.*

This is an outrage. Americans were never meant to endure such abuse, such coercion, such oppression, such tyranny.

In 1913, when the income tax was created, those earning more than $20,000 and less than $50,000 paid 1 percent. Those earning more than $50,000 paid 1 percent on the amount they earned between $20,000 and $50,000 and 2 percent on the income above $50,000. It went up to 3 percent over $75,000, 4 percent over $100,000, 5 percent over $250,000, and there was a top rate of 6 percent over $500,000.

In 1913, a person was considered wealthy with an annual income of $20,000. That was the equivalent of roughly $200,000 in 2000.

Fewer than 5 percent of Americans paid any taxes at all under the original scheme. In other words, 95 percent did not earn $20,000 and were thus exempt. That's how it was ushered in relatively quietly—without much meaningful protest.

Today, many Americans pay nearly 50 percent of their incomes to the federal government. Most never even see the money. It is paid directly to the government by their employers so they won't even miss it—so they won't even comprehend the magnitude of the fraud being perpetrated. Even worse, in principle, Congress has the authority to levy a 100 percent tax on Americans anytime it wishes. In fact, the income tax has ranged as high as 94 percent in war times.

Principle is paramount. If the government has the right to your money—as much of it as it wants—then, in reality, you own nothing.

An unsung hero of American politics saw the scam from inside and decided he wanted nothing to do with it. His name was T. Coleman Andrews, and as W. Cleon Skousen details in *The Making of America*, during the 1950s Andrews served for three years as commissioner of the Internal Revenue Service before resigning in protest at the injustice he witnessed firsthand.

"Congress (in implementing the Sixteenth Amendment) went beyond merely enacting an income tax law and repealed Article IV of the Bill of Rights, by empowering the tax collector to do the very things from which that article says we were to be secure," said Andrews. "It opened up our homes, our papers and our effects to the prying eyes of government agents and set the stage for searches of our books and vaults and inquiries into our private affairs whenever the tax men might decide, even though there might not be any justification beyond mere cynical suspicion."

The founders warned repeatedly about the concept of a direct tax except in a dire emergency such as war. Even under those circumstances, they believed such a tax should never be levied according to wealth. Why? Coleman explains in his insightful resignation statement.

"As matters now stand, if our children make the most of their capabilities and training they will have to give most of it to the tax collector and so become slaves of the government," he said. "People cannot pull themselves up by their own bootstraps anymore because the tax collector gets the boots and the straps as well. The income tax is bad because it is oppressive to all and discriminates particularly against those people who prove themselves most adept at keeping the wheels of business turning and creating maximum employment and high standards of living for their fellow men."

I love Coleman's closing statement. Let it be the belated battle cry of the Second War of Independence. Fifty years later, let our ears be opened: "I believe that a better way to raise revenue not only can be found but must be found, because I am convinced that the present system is leading us right back to the very tyranny from which those, who established this land of freedom, risked their lives, their fortunes and their sacred honor to forever free themselves."

Are you coming to the realization that, like your heroic forefathers, you are being subjected to taxation without meaningful representation? Is there any doubt the income tax is more burdensome, more onerous, more painful, more oppressive, and less fair than the little tax on tea or the Stamp Act that set off our founders?

America will never again be a free country until it ends the income tax. I'll bet you agree with that statement. I'll bet a referendum on ending the income tax would be approved by 75 percent of the American people—maybe 90 percent.

Yet most of us throw up our hands and think it will never happen. It can't happen, we think. The government has become too big and too reliant on that revenue. Too many people are themselves reliant— or think they are—on checks from the government, money literally confiscated by force from their friends, their neighbors, their own family members.

Somebody has to stand up and just say no. Letters to members of Congress aren't good enough. Too many members of Congress are afraid to take on the Internal Revenue Service for fear the monster will come after them. It's going to take a grassroots rebellion—the kind envisioned by our founders when, as they saw it, government would inevitably assume too much power from the people.

In actuality, the federal government derives so much revenue from so many sources it could easily perform all of its constitutional functions (and even some extraconstitutional roles) with revenues just from non-IRS sources.

The government would not collapse if the IRS and the tax code were scrapped tomorrow. The only thing that would change is that the government would be forced to be prudent, to examine how it is throwing your money around, to stop all the unconstitutional wealth-transfer schemes that are only designed to maintain excessive power in Washington.

Less than *half* of federal revenues are actually derived from individual income taxes. Did you know that? It's amazing, isn't it? Of the fiscal year 2000 tax revenue collected—more than $2 *trillion*—just over $1 trillion came from individual income taxes. You could operate the government at 1990 levels of spending—which were, even then, totally out of control without the income taxes collected in 2000.

A look at the budget figures points out some other problems.

Social Security taxes constitute one-third of federal revenues. That is how Washington claims to have huge budget surpluses, when, in fact, it is still bleeding red ink. If, indeed, we have a surplus, ask yourself, why is the national debt continuing to grow? Why did Congress again vote in 2002 to raise the debt limit?

Only a tiny portion of federal income is derived from tariffs—seen by the founders as the primary constitutional vehicle for raising revenue for the national government. In fact, this was the main source of revenue for Washington through the early part of the twentieth century.

We've come a long way since 1913, haven't we?

Think about that. Think about the millions of hours of productive time the IRS forms waste.

Think about the outrageous intrusion these rules cause into the personal affairs of Americans.

Think about the inherent unfairness of a tax system that applies different standards to different people based on their incomes.

Think about the government's unspoken threat of force and violence that accompanies this process.

Think about what little say Americans have about the tax system.

Think about how government wastes, misuses, and illegally redistributes the revenues it collects.

Think about how the system confiscates your wealth before you even see it—by forcing employers to do government's dirty work.

Think about how some people are forced to pay up to 50 percent of their income to government.

Think about how little Americans know—or could possibly know—about a tax code written by lawyers for lawyers and encompassing thousands of pages that few could digest in a lifetime of study.

Think about how close to 50 percent of the American people have been dropped completely from the tax rolls, while the other half is forced into indentured servitude.

Think about how our confiscatory tax system has forced millions of homes to send both parents into the workplace and turn their kids over as the wards of the state schools and MTV.

Think about how Americans are conditioned to accept it blindly, like sheep led to slaughter.

I'd like to get Americans thinking about all of this. It's way past time for Americans to wake up, rise up, and say, "Enough is enough. We demand our government back."

Our founders fought a war for independence more than two hundred years ago over grievances far less threatening to individual freedom and self-government than those Americans face today. It's time for a new declaration of independence. It's time for rebellion. It's time, frankly, for revolution.

You may say, "Farah, there just aren't enough Americans as angry as you are about this injustice, this servitude to government, this slavery. Americans are too comfortable, with their two televisions and two cars in the garage. They are not going to rise up angry and take their government back anytime soon."

You might be right. But then again, I recall that the patriot movement in 1776 was a minority cause. There were far more colonists who thought life under British tyranny was at least tolerable. The majority was comfortable—just as it is today. They were fat and lazy—I'm just not sure if they were as stupid as we are today.

As I've said before, being informed is the first step to achieving and maintaining freedom. Only an educated and moral people can aspire to be free. That's why I wrote this book—to remind Americans about the important things, to remind them of their heritage, to remind them what freedom is, to remind them how precious independence and self-government are.

The income tax is a great place to start taking America back. It's time for people not just to protect themselves by careful financial and tax planning, but actually to grapple with the government directly in an effort to overturn the entire system. Yes, of course, minimize what you pay the government by every legal means. But challenge your government to prove the constitutionality of the system. Don't believe the propaganda that good citizenship means willingly and cheerfully paying whatever arbitrary tax rate is imposed upon you. In America, good citizens obey the Constitution and hold their elected leaders accountable to it.

Good citizenship in America, first and foremost, requires us to end the income tax and close down the IRS.

It will be an uphill fight. Remember how I told you that back in 1913 when the income tax was launched, only 5 percent of Americans were required to file? There was a reason for that. The income tax was billed as a tax on the rich. That's why and how it was approved—though, many contend, illegally.

Today, about 80 percent of Americans are required to file. Why don't they rebel? Because about half of Americans pay little or no taxes at all. Government has created a stratified society of producers and nonproducers—givers and takers. Government utilizes the political muscle of the nonproducers, the takers, to soak the producers, the givers.

It's quite a racket.

You might notice that each new "tax reform" approved by Congress drops more citizens from the tax rolls. The latest Bush plan, for instance, boasts of dropping one in five families—about six million.

On the face of it, that may seem like a good thing. But it's not. What's wrong with dropping more families from the tax rolls? It plays right into the hands of the class-warfare strategists who have pushed confiscatory rates upon the most productive sector of the economy. Let me explain.

According to IRS statistics, before the Bush plan was implemented—the top 1 percent of American income earners paid a disproportionate 34.8 percent of federal tax dollars. These are not necessarily millionaires, folks. The income threshold for that rate is $269,496. That figure may represent a lot of money in many parts of the country, but for those of us who live in New York, Washington, San Francisco, and other areas where the cost of living is high, $269,496 doesn't go as far as you might think.

While paying 34.8 percent of the tax load, these working families actually earn only 18.5 percent of the income. Compare the burden of this 1 percent to the share paid by the bottom 50 percent of taxpayers. They pay only 4.2 percent of federal taxes collected—even though they earn 13.7 percent of the income.

This is just one reason a "progressive" income tax is so unfair. It must be abolished. We must change the culture's attitude toward this socialistic idea or it will represent—and I don't exaggerate—the end of our free republic.

Think about some more numbers. Those earning $100,000 a year or more—hardly a fortune these days—have paid more than 70 percent of individual income taxes.

But under the Bush plan the productive people pay an even larger share of the tax burden. Instead of carrying a 70 percent burden, that group will bear a 74.2 percent load! In other words, the productive people will get soaked even more—at least in terms of the percentages paid. In essence, after implementation of the Bush plan, 50 percent of the public will be paying no taxes, while the other half of the population carries their extra weight.

Now, what does that mean pragmatically in a free society? It means it will be even tougher to achieve the only real tax reform that counts—to abolish the income tax, to scrap the tax code, to dismantle the IRS. You see, half the population will be getting, in essence, a free ride. They can then dictate to the other half. They can set the rules of even more intense class warfare. They can, in effect, further enslave the productive class.

When the thirteen colonies were still a part of the British Empire, Professor Alexander Tyler, a Scottish historian, wrote about the Athenian Republic more than two thousand years earlier: "A democracy cannot exist as a permanent form of government. It can only exist until the voters discover that they can vote themselves money from the public treasury. From that moment on, the majority always votes for the candidates promising the most money from the public treasury, with the result that a democracy always collapses over loose fiscal policy followed by a dictatorship."

That's right. Wealth redistribution programs won't work for very long. They never do. That kind of system destroys itself—always. It's just a matter of time. And that's where we are headed unless the American people rise up angry and take their government back.

Let me give you some more numbers to put this national scandal in perspective: One-fourth of all those who filed tax returns in 1998 paid no income taxes at all. Meanwhile, the top 10 percent of taxpayers paid 63 percent of individual income taxes, up from 49 percent in 1980.

We're all familiar with the fact that individuals work on average from January through May just to pay the government. Only in June through December do taxpayers get the chance to work for themselves.

Less known, however, is the fact that "tax freedom day" for businesses actually comes much later than May. A survey of business taxation in 1999 by Carl Olson of the Fund for Stockowners Rights, shows that the average business serves the state until September 5. In addition to income taxes, businesses pay payroll taxes, property taxes, sales taxes, utility taxes and more. Altogether, according to Olson's survey of 115 major corporations, total taxes averaged a staggering 213 percent of 1999 net incomes.

The highest tax percentage found by Olson was by Burlington Resources, which paid $131 million in taxes while ending up with $1 million in net income. That's 13,100 percent! Ascent Assurance paid 2,250 percent; Texaco, 672 percent; Cabot Oil & Gas, 435 percent; and International Paper, 356 percent. As WorldNetDaily.com reported in January 2001, Winn-Dixie Stores felt so strongly about its tax burden that it publicized it on the front cover of its 1999 annual report: "Earnings per diluted share $1.23. Taxes per diluted share $2.07."

What do you call this? Bad economic policy? I call it slavery to the state.

Taxation and regulation are strangling production, innovation, research, social advancement, and yes, freedom. When are the American people going to wake up? When are U.S. business leaders going to stand up and be counted?

Socialism is alive and well in the United States of America. And it will take more than a little tax cut to get the country back on track. We shouldn't be talking about modest tax reductions. We ought to be talking about the elimination of taxes altogether—particularly the income tax.

Here are some more facts about our so-called "progressive" income tax:

The top 25 percent of taxpayers (based on earnings) paid 80 percent of all federal individual income taxes. And who were those people? They qualified if they had an adjusted gross income of only $44,200.

In 1997, the per-capita federal tax burden was 44 percent higher than in 1992. It was 65 percent higher than in 1988.

Washington doesn't tax your dollars once; it taxes them over and over and over again. Parents can't help children with down payments on a house without the government taking a cut. Children can't repay their parents' generosity without tax implications. Businesses often must be sold upon the death of a founder because of the tax system. All this attention on dollars that have already been taxed previously.

It's time to wake up, America. It's time to just say, "No more." The idea of the "progressive" tax is socialism, pure and simple. And you can see how it works to empower the state and disenfranchise the individual in America today.

It sounds great in theory, which is why government schools begin indoctrinating kids on the logic of the progressive tax in elementary school. The concept is that those earning more not only pay more in real dollars, but in higher percentages as well. This is supposed to be "fair," because the wealthy can afford to pay more.

In reality, what always happens in such systems is that you create political class warfare. The highest earners and the most productive people in society bear an increasingly greater share of the burden of operating government. Government's main role becomes the redistribution of this wealth—taking it from the rich and giving it to the poor, always, of course, with an 80 percent cut going to administer this legalized thievery.

In 2000, U.S. taxpayers were paying a higher percentage of gross domestic product than anytime since World War II. Most people didn't complain and it scarcely became an issue in the presidential campaign because most people are not paying taxes. About 50 percent of the public—earning, say, below $30,000 a year—pay next to nothing, or about 3 percent of the total raised by the federal government.

In other words, 97 percent of the tax money is extorted from the top 50 percent of taxpayers. I use the term *extorted* advisedly. Just try not paying the so-called "voluntary" income tax if you think we're not paying it at the point of a gun.

I'll bet 90 percent of those reading my words right now fall into that top 50 percent. Did you realize you were one of the "rich folks" who have been getting off too easily and not doing your share to help the less fortunate? One of the games played in Washington today is to get more voters dependent on government in one way or another, so that they can control elections by simply squeezing more money out of the productive sector of society—creating virtual serfs of the most productive workers.

Taxes have a long and bloody history in the world. The Scriptures warn us about tax collectors and other sinners repeatedly. But one such reference, in one of the most popular stories in the Bible, is often overlooked.

Luke 2 begins:

> And it came to pass in those days, that there went out a decree from Caesar Augustus, that all the world should be taxed. (And this taxing was first made when Cyrenius was governor of Syria.) And all went to be taxed, every one into his own city. And Joseph also went up from Galilee, out of the city of Nazareth, into Judaea, unto the city of David, which is called Bethlehem; (because he was of the house and lineage of David:) to be taxed with Mary his espoused wife, being great with child. And so it was, that, while they were there, the days were accomplished that she should be delivered. (vv. 1–6)

Notice how many times the subject of taxes comes up in that first section of the Christmas story. That was the reason Joseph and Mary were forced to travel to Bethlehem from their home in Nazareth, a rough journey of about seventy miles for a young woman in her ninth month of pregnancy. They had to file their 1040 form.

It ought to be referred to as "the Long March to Bethlehem," because of its familiarity with the forced population movements of so many modern-day tyrannies. Jesus' birth was marked by the first world tax. The Roman Empire was ready, willing, and able to coerce millions of people throughout the world to battle the elements, to travel great distances, regardless of their conditions, so that they could be counted and taxed. No excuses were tolerated. This was a government operation all the way.

Some modern-day shakedown artists like Jesse Jackson like to suggest that Jesus and Mary were homeless people. Not true. Note the next verse: "And she brought forth her firstborn son, and wrapped him in swaddling clothes, and laid him in a manger; because there was no room for them in the inn" (Luke 2:7). Joseph was a carpenter, a workingman, who had money for a room at the inn in Bethlehem. It's just that there were no vacancies due to the overcrowded conditions caused by this forced population relocation.

Government is not your friend. It is the enemy of freedom. Government is not Santa Claus. It is the Grinch. Government is not your servant. It tends all too often to be our master. Government seldom helps people. It often enslaves them.

Even two thousand years ago, government was heartless and cruel. It forced women to march long distances in the last stages of pregnancy. That's the way government has always been and that's the way it will always be—at least until Jesus comes again. Our job as free people in the meantime is to control it—to make ourselves as free as possible by limiting government's reach.

What about the poor? What about the needy? A young lady wrote to me asking what I think should be done with regard to "the problems of the poor" in our newly liberated America.

"After all," she wrote, "you criticize various plans for government intervention to help poor people. Instead of telling people what you don't like, why not tell us what you would do, or how you think government should act?"

This question, of course, assumes that there is something government can and/or should do to address the inability or unwillingness of individuals to support themselves and their families. I believe most everything government does in this regard is counterproductive and immoral.

But if I were made king for the day, my first action would be to eliminate the income tax, which is the single biggest barrier to wealth creation faced by Americans today. I would also repeal all laws that regulate commerce between individuals—including, but not limited to, the minimum-wage requirement.

Free people have the right to work for whatever wage is acceptable to them. Free people have the right to make agreements between themselves without the government getting involved, establishing ground rules and cutting themselves in for a piece of the action. Free people have the right to collect their wages without government confiscating a percentage of their wealth in advance.

How would such reforms help the poor? Instead of subsidizing poverty and slothfulness, as the U.S. government does with its many and varied wealth-redistribution schemes, this action would remove the heavy baggage of government from the backs of millions of the most productive people. Thus, the action would create incentives to be self-supportive as opposed to creating incentives not to work.

Is that enough? Not by a long shot. No economic system can solve the problems that are problems of the heart and soul. No economic system can hold families together. No economic system can miraculously inspire people to become more loving and charitable. But we must begin by removing the disincentives, and there are many in our increasingly socialist system that turn individual problems into societal problems.

Taking America back means persuading married couples that both adults in the family do not have to work—and that the best way to raise their children and create a happy and productive home is for one of them to stay home. Over the last forty years, American women have been coerced into the workplace. It's not a matter of choice for many. Because the income tax takes such a bite out of the family earnings, many husbands and wives feel they have no alternative but to both join the workforce. Feminism has been used as a sociological rationalization for this trend. If women are not working, they are told, they are not "liberated."

Nonsense.

There's nothing compassionate about forcing both parents to work.

It is in our best interests as a society if one parent stays home to rear children. That has always been the case.

Kids are no longer supervised by parents. They are supervised for six, seven, eight hours a day by government employees. Now government is moving to ensure that even preschoolers are cared for by government employees—anyone but parents.

Government, through heavy taxation, has created the need for both parents to enter the workforce. Now government, which created the problem in the first place, comes up with plans to solve the problem, which in reality will only worsen it.

Shouldn't we stop looking to government to put Band-Aids on injuries it has inflicted? Wouldn't it be better if one parent had the option of staying home to take care of kids because a single income was enough to support a family? That's the way it used to be in America. That's the way it ought to be. That's the way it can be again if we get government off our backs and out of our pockets.

And yes, that's the beginning of my answer as to how we can really help the poor in America—and begin taking America back.

What Americans must realize if they are to get their country back is that every new government program means less freedom, less control over their own property, less control over their own lives, less control over their own families—and more dependence.

It's time to stand up and resist. Don't wait for the leaders to emerge on this movement. It won't happen. You are the leader. Others will follow. Don't do as you're told. You tell your government what to do. That's the way it is supposed to work in America.

If 10 or 20 percent of Americans challenged the IRS, this battle would be over. Then we'd be on to the next battle—taking our families back.

★ 8 ★

NUKING THE NUCLEAR FAMILY

Marriage is honourable in all, and the bed undefiled: but whore-mongers and adulterers God will judge.

—HEBREWS 13:4

WESTERN CIVILIZATION WOULD HAVE BEEN IMPOSSIBLE without the nuclear family as the building block.

Does anyone dispute that statement?

So, why is the family under attack like never before?

Because Western civilization—and the entire notion of self-government that emerged from it—is the real target.

Karl Marx, the father of Communism, understood that for his evil ideology to succeed it would require the elimination of the family structure, in which parents are accountable to God and children accountable to parents.

Today, while many Americans labor under the delusion that Marx's utopian dreams are dead, the remnants of Western civilization, led by this once-great country, have been seduced by statists who seek to steal our children and make a mockery of the family.

They do this in innumerable ways, but here are a few:

- by persuading us that "alternative lifestyles" are just as good as the institution of marriage;
- by persuading us that the state should take the central role in educating children;
- by persuading us that the killing of unborn children is a valid choice for pregnant women, one that should even be supported by tax subsidies;
- by persuading us that both parents should work outside of the home;
- by persuading us that children, even small ones, develop just as well when cared for by strangers in group situations as they do when raised by parents;
- by sexualizing our children at younger and younger ages;
- by convincing us that there's nothing we can do about the increasingly high divorce rate in this country and that divorce doesn't necessarily hurt children.

To listen to the advocates of same-sex marriages, you would believe that homosexuals are being denied their civil rights because they cannot marry one another. The fact that such a notion is even being entertained in the media and in public policy debates today illustrates just how demented our culture has become.

Can you imagine having this debate ten or twenty years ago? Of course not. The idea of men marrying men and women marrying women would have been dismissed as quickly as the idea of men marrying sheep. In fact, that's not a bad analogy with which to begin dissecting this issue.

For a moment, let's wave a magic wand and pretend we can actually grant the same-sex marriage advocates their wish. "Bibbidi-Bobbidi-Boo." *Poof!* Same-sex marriages are now legal. Marriage is no longer an institution between one man and one woman. Now women can marry women and men can marry men.

Why stop there?

After all, the same-sex marriage advocates tell us the only reason marriage remains an institution for heterosexual couples is because of archaic religious ideas. If those ideas—the very foundation of Western civilization—are going out the window, then on to the next taboo.

What about marriage between brothers and sisters? Fathers and daughters? Mothers and sons? Brothers and brothers? Any problems yet?

The standard reply you get when you pose this challenge to the same-sex marriage advocates is that you are being absurd—there's just no demand out there for such unions. To which I say, So what? There was no demand for same-sex marriages just a few years ago. Surely there are people in the world who wish very sincerely to follow their hearts and form marital unions such as those described above. You can probably see them on daytime television right now.

Furthermore, is it simply market demand that makes such unions right? When enough people no longer feel squeamish about incest, will it be time to break down that barrier?

Let's go a step further. Since marriage is no longer an institution exclusively joining one woman with one man, isn't it time to reconsider polygamy? Hello? How can we in good conscience tell a man who sincerely wants five wives he can't have them? It's part of his makeup. It's who he is. He was born that way with a predilection against monogamy. Can you stifle his rights and those of his consenting would-be adult wives?

But then again, why limit these unions to adults? Isn't that just part of that old archaic religious notion that only adults should experience the pleasures of marriage? Why shouldn't children be allowed to marry? Isn't that age discrimination?

Which brings us back to where we started. The only taboo left at that point will be marriages outside the species. How can we deny a man or woman the right to form a domestic partnership with a domestic animal? It's just not right.

You see, we're losing common sense when we sanction homosexual marriages. To do so is to redefine marriage. If homosexuals want to get together and create a new institution that celebrates their love and commitment to one another, they are free to do that. Let's just not call it *marriage*, because that changes the definition of a word and a sacred six-thousand-year-old institution.

Likewise, it's important to remember that homosexuals are defined as such because of their behavior, their sexual activity, and their proclivities. No other group of people in our society is awarded special recognition and protection because of their behavior or inclinations.

If we continue down this road, then we'll have to be sure not to discriminate against adulterers, drunks, smokers—eventually even pedophiles. Once you start moving that line, you can't stop.

And let's remember the principal reason for the institution of marriage. It's the union of two people that forms the basis of another important institution—the family. What kind of families will we create with these bold new unions proposed by the same-sex marriage advocates? Do you think the kids adopted into such families will really get the benefits motherhood and fatherhood offer?

The fact that there is even serious discussion about this idea among people not currently under psychiatric care is scary—downright scary.

Perhaps nothing better illustrates this strange phenomenon than the war on the Boy Scouts.

Just a few years ago, we can all remember, the Boy Scouts of America was seen universally as an upstanding organization that epitomized everything wholesome about American youth. It was a group that taught good values to boys. It was a group that selflessly offered great opportunities for learning. It was a group known for promoting good deeds, virtue, and important skills. It was a group that seemed about as nonthreatening and noncontroversial as any in the world.

Today it is under concerted attack—from organized atheists, from orga-nized homosexual activists, from radical feminists, and, worst of all, from government and the courts.

Why would the Boy Scouts go from pillar of respectability to subversive organization in one generation?

A Boy Scout pledges to be trustworthy, loyal, helpful, friendly, courteous, kind, obedient, cheerful, thrifty, brave, clean, and reverent. A Boy Scout vows to keep himself physically strong, morally straight, and mentally alert.

Because of these characteristics and goals, the Boy Scouts are under siege. When you see an institution like this under attack, it should set off an internal warning that our very way of life—not just the Boy Scouts—is threatened by an organized, well-funded conspiracy. I know many do not like that word *conspiracy*, but no other synonym in the English language is appropriate in this context.

Think about it.

We must come to grips with the fact that there are people in our society today who believe that it is unconstitutional for citizens to act on their moral judgments. They believe that the state has the right coercively to dictate conscience. And they will use all of their power, time, energy, and resources to remake America as they see fit.

It is a conspiracy. It has an ultimate goal, which is hidden. It has interim objectives, which often seem innocuous. It uses the slow-boiling frog method of transforming society as its strategy. The way of life that most Americans take for granted is at stake.

Let me show you what I mean. Remember when the homosexual political movement began? We were told that it was only about what people do in the privacy of their own bedrooms. After all, who could argue that sexuality was a private matter—that it was none of the government's business what people did with their bodies in the most intimate and private settings? Sexual behavior, the advocates explained, was *nobody* else's business.

Once that victory was achieved and a consensus was established, however, new goals, new objectives emerged.

No longer is sexual behavior a private matter. Now the advocates of the homosexual movement are the very same people who are making sexuality a public matter—teaching their practices in schools, criminalizing "discrimination" against those who practice it, flaunting the most aberrant behavior in parades and on city streets, and demanding that the rest of us accept it, condone it, and celebrate it.

As these enemies of freedom, morality, and responsibility see it, the Boy Scouts do not have the right to assert their most basic First Amendment rights—to assemble, to hold certain principles, to express their views, and to promote virtuous behavior.

Let's be clear about the terms of this debate. I do not seek to deny homosexuals any of their God-given, unalienable civil rights. Neither do the Boy Scouts. Rather, it is the homosexual political activists who seek to undermine the institutions that represent the bedrock of freedom, of self-government, of individual rather than group rights.

And they are succeeding. As incredible as it may seem, they are winning this battle. The establishment press is their ally. The entertainment industry is their ally. The federal government is their ally. The schools are their allies. The foundations are their allies. Even many of the apostate churches and synagogues are their allies.

Here is just a sampling of the way this war is being fought:

I did a Lexis-Nexis search (www.LexisNexis.com) and found only a handful of commentaries by national figures who have stood up and proudly proclaimed their unequivocal support for the Boy Scouts in their battles with homosexual activists and atheists who seek to change the very character of the organization.

Meanwhile, just look at those attacking the Scouts:

A few years ago, the Clinton administration launched an investigation of the Scouts' ties to federal agencies with an eye toward disallowing the use of national parks and military installations for jamborees.

Vice President Gore said he would like to see a law passed that would force the Scouts to accommodate homosexuals. And he won the popular vote for the presidency after making that absurd comment.

Some two dozen United Way chapters cut off the Scouts from all funding.

The Los Angeles City Council voted unanimously to evict the Scouts from public facilities.

The Broward County school board in Florida voted unanimously to evict sixty troops and Cub Scout packs.

In Dade County, Florida; Santa Barbara, California; and

Minneapolis, Minnesota, Scouts were told to halt all recruiting drives in schools and prohibited from handing out literature.

Knight Ridder, Inc. and Levi Strauss cut off funding to the Boy Scouts.

Church groups within at least four major Christian denominations passed resolutions condemning the Scouts' policy against homosexual behavior.

Together, those institutions and others represent a powerful force pushing our culture. There are few courageous souls willing to push back—to endure the inevitable criticism, ridicule, and intimidation that follow.

It's time to reframe the debate. That's the only way our civilization as we know it can survive. It's time to tell the truth. That's the only way we will be able to take American back. It's time to stand up for decency.

Look at what happens to those who dare to do that. Dr. Laura Schlessinger, one of America's most successful radio personalities, stood up for common sense on this issue. She has been the target of ruthless attacks and smears ever since.

That we now live in a world in which it is dangerous to stand up for trustworthiness, loyalty, helpfulness, friendliness, courtesy, kindness, obedience, cheerfulness, bravery, cleanliness, and reverence should be a warning to us all.

The stakes are high.

I'm standing up to join the enemies list. You need to do so too. I support the Boy Scouts—unequivocally, unabashedly, unashamedly, and without reservation. The Boy Scouts personify the kind of world in which I would like to live and raise my family.

If this is the new dividing line in our society, let the barricades be erected. I'm not retreating—not another inch. But not retreating is, as I have pointed out in earlier chapters, still a recipe for defeat. We need to take ground back in this war. We need to take the offense. We need to begin taking America back.

We in America have come to believe that "discrimination" is always a bad thing. Right? I bet many people reading this book right now think about "discrimination" as a negative characteristic entirely.

Discrimination is not a bad thing. In fact, I daresay none of us could survive very long without discriminating every single day. We are constantly faced with choices in daily life. We have to make decisions. Every time we make a choice, we are guilty of discriminating. Not only is there nothing *wrong* with this process, but it is the essential element of responsible behavior.

We all discriminate. We choose to do certain things and not to do others. We choose to associate with certain people and not to associate with others. We choose to believe in certain principles and not to believe in others. I don't think any of us could live a healthy and productive life full of choices without discriminating between those that are good for us and those that are bad for us.

I teach my kids to discriminate. I tell them which foods are healthy and which are not. If they did not exercise discrimination, they would probably eat nothing but chocolate and ice cream. I teach them some things are right and some things are wrong. Without discriminating between right and wrong, we become amoral people.

So let us agree that "discrimination" is not necessarily a bad thing.

Discrimination, though, is the central indictment against the Boy Scouts. It is the high crime for which the group stands accused. It is the reason courts are ruling against the organization and why local, state, and federal governments are taking a new look at its activities.

Let's face it: The very name *Boy* Scouts suggests discrimination, does it not? This organization is not the Scouts. It is the *Boy* Scouts. Thus, no one can pretend that this is an organization that is all-inclusive, that it is meant for everyone. Instead, it is a private organization with a specific mission—to provide *boys* with an enriching and wholesome experience.

It is not for girls, nor does it seek to compel all boys to participate. It is a voluntary organization—one that has nothing to do with sexual activities of any kind.

Can discrimination be a bad thing? Yes. I teach my kids not to discriminate—meaning to show preference, partiality, or prejudice—against people because of their race. I think racial discrimination is a bad thing—whether it is racial discrimination against black people, brown people, or white people. It is wrong. Period.

But that does not mean that all forms of discrimination—meaning "to make distinctions"—is bad. The ability to make distinctions is a requirement of self-governing free people. Otherwise, we allow others to make distinctions and choices for us.

There are good reasons for the Boy Scouts to ban homosexual scoutmasters. I don't have any boys, but if I did, I would not allow my kids to join if they were supervised by homosexuals. Nor would I allow my girls to join an organization supervised by lesbians.

Why? Do I think all homosexuals are predators? No. But some are. That's why the Girl Scouts don't allow men to supervise their members—because some, perhaps even a tiny minority of men—are predators, and give in to their lust for little girls.

The same self-evident principle applies to Boy Scouts. Men who have an express sexual preference for members of the same sex should never be placed in positions that give them power and authority over boys.

Frankly, that I have to state such an obvious fact in the twenty-first century is frightening to me. But if we are going to take America back we need to set the debate straight. We need to begin at the beginning, with what were once self-evident truths. So I will say it loud and clear: Homosexual men should be kept away from boys—not because they are all predators but because *some* are. If that's discrimination, count me in. If that's against the law, the law is wrong. If that's in opposition to the majority opinion, I don't care. That's the attitude we must have if we are to take America back.

We need to think of the children first. Their protection must be paramount. No one has a God-given right to supervise children. That is a privilege that must be earned. It is a position of trust. It is nothing short of insanity to turn children over to supervisors and authority figures who would be tempted sexually to corrupt and abuse them. Sex is not a part of the Boy Scout mission. And those who seek to turn this organization into a political whipping boy because of the commonsense principles it upholds are worse than despicable. They are misguided. They are dangerous. They are evil. They threaten not only one of the greatest private organizations in the United States, but our entire culture—our ability to think clearly, our sense of morality, our ideas about right and wrong.

They threaten your family.

Here's a question to ask anyone who criticizes the Boy Scouts for its stand on homosexual scoutmasters: Would he or she knowingly hire a self-proclaimed, practicing homosexual baby-sitter to care for his or her own children? Whatever the public answer is to that question, I sincerely doubt anyone in his or her right mind would.

Here's another test question to pose: Would you rather live in a community populated mostly by Boy Scouts and Scout leaders or one populated mostly by members of ACT-UP?

Now, as much as I personally detest the radical homosexual activist organization ACT-UP and everything for which it stands, I'm not campaigning to shut down the extremist group. I'm not even advocating coercion through government or outside pressure on its leadership to accept as members heterosexuals who don't believe in its philosophy.

Why? Because I believe in freedom. And freedom is a concept the enemies of the Boy Scouts simply don't understand, appreciate, or respect.

If you agree with me that living in a community heavily salted with Boy Scouts would be preferable to living in a community infested with ACT-UP types, then you need to make your voice heard. You need to stand up and be counted. You need to support the Boy Scouts of America in every way you can.

And you need to be the enemy of those attacking this vital and honorable organization. You need to start taking back your community. You need to start standing up for what's right. You need to take back your church. You need to withdraw your children from the clutches of those who would victimize them. You need to protect your family. That's how we take America back—one house, one community, one church, one city at a time.

We'll never take America back unless we use the nuclear family as the building block, just as our founders did.

What's the definition of a family? Quite simple. It is two or more people living together related by marriage, blood, or adoption. This is why the homosexual activists are so eager to legitimize homosexual marriages and homosexual adoptions. If they are successful, they will no longer have to destroy the family. It will have been destroyed by redefinition.

Think about it. Do you remember reading about the man in Utah who was convicted of bigamy? He had five wives and twenty-nine children. Last I heard, he was facing twenty-five years in prison.

Keep in mind he didn't force any of his wives to marry him. While he was fifty-two when he came to national attention, his wives ranged in age from twenty-four to thirty-one—all consenting adults. Utah officials went after him following media appearances he made last year on *Dateline* and *Jerry Springer*. Polygamy was outlawed in Utah, a state heavily populated by members of the Church of Jesus Christ of Latter-day Saints, which once permitted the practice.

Now, I'm not particularly fond of polygamy. In fact, I detest the practice. I abhor it. I believe it to be a sin. Granted, some biblical figures— kings and the like—received special dispensation to have multiple wives, but the Bible, in context, seems clear on the fact that a man was destined to leave his parents and "cleave to his *wife*," not *wives*.

But let me play the devil's advocate here and ask Utah state officials just why this polygamist is being discriminated against for simply living an "alternative lifestyle"? And while I'm at it, let me throw this question out there to all those proponents of other "alternative lifestyles": What do you folks think about this Utah case? And why haven't I heard you rallying to the polygamist's defense?

I'll tell you why: Because polygamists don't have the lobbying power that homosexuals do. It's that simple. And that's how America decides what is right and wrong today—based on public-opinion polls and the clout of narrow, special-interest groups.

Frankly, there is little difference in my eyes between polygamy and homosexuality—except perhaps that there are far more biblical injunctions against homosexuality and in far stronger terms and without any exceptions. It was once true in America that our laws were based on such things as the Ten Commandments and biblical law. That is no longer the case. Today it is simply based on which way the wind is blowing. And the wind is to the backs of the homosexual/transsexual/cross-gendered lobby and in the face of people like the polygamist.

Why? Are there no eternal truths anymore? Is there no right and wrong? Is it all just a question of pop-culture whim?

Today homosexuals not only are a protected class of people based on their sexual behavior, but they are a celebrated group of people on television, in movies, in books, and in the media. They are portrayed as heroes, quite literally. And what places them in that category is what they do in their bedrooms—and sometimes in public rest rooms. That's not right.

Why doesn't our culture also hold up other people as special protected classes based on their sexual proclivities? Let's take adulterers, for example. Hey, I believe men are far more inclined toward adultery and polygamy than women. Some would even tell you that sleeping around is a genetic compulsion.

Yet I have not seen one state or municipality draft laws protecting this class of people—a group, I would suggest, that represents far more constituents than does the homosexual lobby. Is it just a matter of organization? Is that why the polygamist may be in jail today?

"Well, Farah," some will say at this point, "what are you suggesting? Do you think homosexuals and adulterers should be jailed?"

Actually, no. There are a few I would like to see in jail, but, then again, there are even more politicians I'd like to see behind bars. I would just like to see some common sense exercised by our culture and by our legal system.

I don't think homosexuals should be jailed, but I also don't think their lifestyle should be celebrated. I don't think the government should provide them special legal protections as a class. I don't believe their agenda should be brought into schools. I don't think taxpayer funds should be hijacked for their proselytizing efforts. I don't think their diseases should get more research funding than diseases killing far more people. I don't think they should be recruited under government hiring quotas. In other words, I don't think they should have *any* special rights as a group.

You see, the case for polygamy demonstrates conclusively that our society and our legal system do, indeed, make judgments about morality. So when someone tells you that no one has the right to legislate morality, simply remind him of his plight. In fact, explain that all laws reflect someone's morality.

Personally, I think it's time for us to return to the eternal truths that once upon a time helped make this the greatest, freest country in the world. In fact, it's a must if we are going to take America back.

It's not just the homosexual activists who are turning our nation's morality upside down. The popular culture is just as guilty—if not more so. Just look at daytime and prime-time TV programming—what passes for "entertainment" these days.

Romance and marriage are out while casual sex and low-commitment relationships are in. Is it any wonder we are producing a generation of moral misfits?

A study by Rutgers University's National Marriage Project recently found that, unlike generations before them, young men and women in their twenties are simply not interested in finding marriage partners when they date. What are they looking for? The title of the study says it all: "Sex Without Strings, Relationships Without Rings." The report found that young Americans:

- favor living together as a tryout for marriage or as an alternative to marriage;
- believe sex is fun and needs no strings attached;
- have a fear of divorce;
- see marriage (and divorce) as a potential economic liability.

It's no wonder kids have such poor opinions about marriage. Every year, one million more children are victims of divorce. That's twice the number affected in 1960.

Unfortunately, not enough of these kids are learning from the bad experiences of their parents.

It took thirty years, but the "free love" generation has spawned a disaster in its wake. Not only has the selfishness of the '60s and '70s wrecked so many of the lives of those who experienced it firsthand, but the children of that generation are still paying the price. They pay the price not only in terms of wrecked families, but in a warped worldview of hopelessness and lessened expectations.

You can hardly blame the kids, however. They are simply responding to what they are taught in government schools and through the popular culture on a daily basis.

If Americans really want to do something "for the children," they should worry a little less about gun control, airbag regulations, global warming, lawsuits against tobacco companies, mandatory seat belt laws, and all kinds of other nanny-state preoccupations and figure out how to stop divorcing each other.

I speak from experience. I went through it. My kids endured it. It's hell. I wouldn't wish it on my worst enemy. But it has become an easy answer for too many Americans.

One study of 171 cities with populations over 100,000 even draws a correlation between a municipality's divorce rate and its crime rate. Another study shows how family income drops significantly after divorce. The results are tangible and dramatic and always negative.

I could give you all kinds of reasons why lifetime marriage is better than any alternative—with the possible exception of the monastic life. Lasting marriages produce happier, healthier, smarter kids who tend to succeed in life and create new lasting marriages. Marriages that break up produce despair, poverty, crime, and hopelessness.

I hardly have to tell you about the problems of kids born out of wedlock. Just turn on the local TV news in any major U.S. city and you'll see the results.

But it's not just a matter of economics and data and studies. Nor are the physical and emotional tolls the only issues between men and women and how they create families. There's an even more important reason for working at marriages and learning from them.

Throughout the Bible, the kingdom of heaven is likened to a marriage. It seems that God has given us this often-trying institution as a way for men and women to learn to relate to Him. Someday, if we're exceedingly fortunate, we, both men and women, will be welcomed into the kingdom of heaven as His spouse.

Marriage, I believe, is a practice run for our relationship with God in eternity.

That may sound terribly old-fashioned and sentimental to some. But I don't care. In fact, judging from the way kids are looking at marriage these days, we could definitely do with a more spiritual perspective on relationships.

Of course, we could just continue to teach kids how to put condoms on bananas, explain that they are the accidental result of millions of years of evolution, and provide birth control and abortions on demand.

Which answer do you think will produce better results?

I believe many of the social and moral problems we see in America are a direct result of our cavalier attitude toward life itself—as defined by the tragic and thoroughly extraconstitutional U.S. Supreme Court ruling in 1973 known as *Roe v. Wade*.

The average American has been programmed to believe that abortion, under most circumstances, is legal in America.

I've got news for you. It is and it isn't. True, the Supreme Court did what no court is authorized to do in 1973—it created a new law that served to strike down restrictions on abortion in most of the fifty states. So we have this perception that *Roe v. Wade* is the "law of the land." How many times have you heard that statement? Even opponents of abortion often acknowledge *Roe v. Wade* as "the law of the land." It is not.

Let me explain why, in America, it is impossible for that to be the case.

The Constitution of the United States makes it clear that Congress—and only Congress—writes law. The president can't do it.

And certainly, in a constitutional free republic, the Supreme Court cannot do it.

Furthermore, the author of the Constitution, James Madison, noted in the *Federalist Papers* that the powers delegated to the federal government were few and defined, whereas the powers reserved to the states were numerous and indefinite. Here, for your edification, are his exact words:

> The powers delegated by the proposed Constitution to the federal government are few and defined. Those which are to remain in the State governments are numerous and indefinite. The former will be exercised principally on external objects, as war, peace, negotiation, and foreign commerce; with which last the power of taxation will, for the most part, be connected. The powers reserved to the several States will extend to all the objects which, in the ordinary course of affairs, concern the lives, liberties, and properties of the people, and the internal order, improvement, and prosperity of the State.

The federal government was to be subservient to the states. In fact, it was to owe its very existence to the goodwill of the states. Under no circumstance was the federal government to have any influence or power over them.

Certainly, as the founders envisioned it, one branch of the federal government would never be able to dictate to the legislative bodies of the states.

Thomas Jefferson well understood the way an out-of-control judicial branch could destroy the delicate balance under which the federal government was established.

> It has long been my opinion, and I have never shrunk from its expression... that the germ of dissolution of our federal government is in the Constitution of our Federal Judiciary; an irresponsible body (for impeachment is scarcely a scare crow), working like gravity by night and by day, gaining a little today and a little tomorrow, and advancing

its noiseless step like a thief, over the field of jurisdiction, until all shall be usurped from the States, and the government of all be consolidated into one. To this I am opposed; because, when all government, domestic and foreign, in little as in great things, shall be drawn to Washington as the center of power, it will render powerless the checks of one government on another, and will become as venal and oppressive as the government from which we separated. It will be as in Europe, where every man must be either pike or gudgeon.

Roe v. Wade is, in many ways, the ultimate manifestation of what Jefferson foresaw in his grim prophecy about centralization of power.

If *Roe v. Wade* is indeed, as most Americans think, the law of the land, then the U.S. Constitution is null and void. There is simply no other interpretation.

I for one am not yet willing to concede that the U.S. Constitution is null and void. And for sure I am not willing to say that it should serve as a document to be cited when it is convenient and forgotten when it is not.

If America is to be, as the founders planned, a nation of laws, not men, then how can men, with no authority to make law, dictate the law of the land? That, my friends, is the $64,000 question. And that is precisely what happened in *Roe v. Wade*. Nine men in black robes do not make law. It's that simple. That was not a principle upon which America was founded.

It's about time even the most ardent pro-life activists begin questioning not just the logic of *Roe v. Wade*, but the legitimacy.

And let's not stop at *Roe*. It's time to rein in the judicial branch of government across the board. Because as Jefferson suggested, there's no quicker road to tyranny than to allow nine unaccountable despots to have their way with us.

No matter what the court decided in 1973 or in subsequent rulings, abortion is illegal and unconstitutional, and I will prove it to you.

To understand why, you must begin by doing something few Americans bother with anymore—reading the Preamble to the U.S.

Constitution: "We the people of the United States, in order to form a more perfect union, establish justice, insure domestic tranquility, provide for the common defense, promote the general welfare, and secure the blessings of liberty to ourselves and our posterity, do ordain and establish this Constitution for the United States of America."

Important words, all. But I want you to focus right now on those to whom this document applies. Who are the subjects and beneficiaries of the Constitution, as stated clearly in the Preamble? The answer? ". . . to ourselves and our posterity . . ."

The word *ourselves* in this context refers to those men who wrote it—and to their generation of Americans. *Posterity,* which literally means "descendants" or all succeeding generations, refers in this context to all those Americans *yet unborn.*

Is your great-, great-, great-, great-granddaughter your posterity? Absolutely. Is she born yet? Absolutely not. Does the fact that she is not yet born make her any less your posterity? No.

Now, specifically what rights are ascribed by the Constitution to ourselves and our posterity?

> Amendment V: No person shall be held to answer for a capital, or otherwise infamous crime, unless on a presentment or indictment of a grand jury, except in cases arising in the land or naval forces, or in the militia, when in actual ser-vice in time of war or public danger; nor shall any person be subject for the same offense to be twice put in jeopardy of life or limb; nor shall be compelled in any criminal case to be a witness against himself, nor be deprived of life, liberty, or property, without due process of law; nor shall private property be taken for public use, without just compensation.

Clearly, the Fifth Amendment establishes that our posterity—those yet unborn—shall not be deprived of life without due process.

This same principle was contained in the Declaration of Independence: "We hold these truths to be self-evident, that all men are created equal, that they are endowed by their Creator with certain unalienable Rights, that among these are Life, Liberty, and the pursuit of Happiness."

Life is an inalienable right, which means man can't take it away through laws or through Supreme Court decisions. And just so there is no confusion about this being a limitation only on the federal government, check out the Fourteenth Amendment:

Section 1. All persons born or naturalized in the United States, and subject to the jurisdiction thereof, are citizens of the United States and of the state wherein they reside. No state shall make or enforce any law which shall abridge the privileges or immunities of citizens of the United States; nor shall any state deprive any person of life, liberty, or property, without due process of law; nor deny to any person within its jurisdiction the equal protection of the laws.

Tell me, where is due process for those unborn children sentenced to death while still in the womb?

Some abortion advocates have tried to suggest that *Roe v. Wade*— an arbitrary and capricious attempt by the Supreme Court to exceed its constitutional limitations and legislate—is itself the due process for unborn babies.

Once again, however, the Constitution trumps that poor excuse for an argument:

Amendment VI: In all criminal prosecutions, the accused shall enjoy the right to a speedy and public trial, by an impartial jury of the state and district wherein the crime shall have been committed; which district shall have been previously ascertained by law, and to be informed of the nature and cause of the accusation; to be confronted with the witnesses against him; to have compulsory process for obtaining witnesses in his favor, and to have the assistance of counsel for his defense.

Roe v. Wade is thus a sham—a house of cards. It was an artificial attempt to make abortion a right by citing a "right of privacy" that is itself nowhere to be found in the Constitution. *Roe v. Wade* created rights where none existed and abrogated those that were enshrined as inalienable.

I rest my case.

But I will not rest entirely until this nation is awakened to abortion as both a national tragedy and a constitutional threat to all of our God-given rights—as well as an endangerment to the lives and liberties of our posterity.

That's part of what we must do in taking America back.

LET MY CHILDREN GO

Let divines and philosophers, statesmen, and patriots, unite their endeavors to renovate the age, the impressing the minds of men with the importance of educating their little boys and girls, of inculcating in the minds of youth the fear and love of the Deity and universal philanthropy, and, in subordination to these great principles, the love of their country; of instructing them in the art of self-government, without which they can never act a wise part in the government of societies, great or small; in short, of leading them in the study and practice of the exalted virtues of the Christian system . . .

—SAMUEL ADAMS

My people are destroyed for lack of knowledge: because thou hast rejected knowledge, I will also reject thee, that thou shalt be no priest to me: seeing thou hast forgotten the law of thy God, I will also forget thy children.

—HOSEA 4:6

YOU CAN QUOTE STATISTICS ALL DAY ABOUT THE DIVORCE rate, child abuse, the drug epidemic, and the rising tide of violence in our society. But sometimes you can get a better glimpse of the ethical depths to which our nation has plummeted by examining some individual stories.

On May 1, 1997, eleven-year-old Heather Trelow sat in her Amelia Earhart Elementary School classroom in Alameda, California, and listened to her teacher, Victoria Forrester, lead a discussion about the virtues of the previous night's "coming out" episode of the ABC-TV show *Ellen*.

After praising the program and the lead character as "proud and brave," the teacher asked the children if they agreed with her. Heather was one of only three kids who did not raise their hands. You can imagine how uncomfortable the youngster was when interrogated in class about why she disagreed.

Is this education, or is it indoctrination? Heather's parents believe it was the latter. As the *San Francisco Chronicle* later reported, they pulled her out of the school and asked the state to revoke the license of the fifth-grade teacher.

"The teacher told my daughter later, 'I know how your parents are raising you, but you need to be open to other points of view,'" said Mike Trelow, Heather's father, an avowed Christian who believes homosexual activity is immoral.

If anyone needs to open herself up to other points of view, it's this teacher! She ought to her head examined. How dare someone charged by the state with the responsibility of educating impressionable eleven-year-old minds resort to such brainwashing?

And I say this with the full knowledge that this case is not unusual. In fact, my own children had similar experiences in government schools before we pulled them out. Ms. Forrester is hardly unique, though she certainly ought to be stripped of her teaching credentials. The administrators who have apologized for her behavior ought to be next. And the recall process should be warmed up for those board-of-education members who have publicly determined that this case actually represents an invasion of their turf by right-wing Christian zealots.

"My sense is that this is larger than Alameda," said board member Christine Allen about the case. "Alameda is the type of community right-wing and religious-right groups go after."

Somebody get a net and drop it over that woman's head. Here is a story of a concerned parent simply watching out for his daughter's best interests and trying to shape her moral character without interference from the government morality police—people like Ms. Allen and Ms. Forrester.

Think about it. That's what they are. They think they're openminded, but yet they are totally intolerant of other people's viewpoints.

What's happening in the government schools today is a crime against humanity. There is no other way to describe it. Students are being intentionally dumbed down, indoctrinated into a mindless form of political correctness, conditioned like Pavlov's dogs, and you, the taxpayers, are required to pay more and more and more as test scores drop lower and lower and lower.

An enterprising *San Francisco Examiner* reporter recently conducted an informal survey of what high-school graduates knew about civics and basic U.S. history. The results are enough to make you sick.

Less than half of the teenagers polled could identify the country from which the U.S. won its independence.

Asked what July 4 is all about, one high-school graduate said: "It's like the freedom. Some war was fought and we won, so we got our freedom."

Another was asked which country America fought with in the war for independence: "I want to say Korea."

How long ago was this war fought? "Like fifty years."

The governmentalization of education in this country is a total, unequivocal failure.

It's actually quite a recent phenomenon that governments at every level—from towns and villages to counties and states, and, increasingly, Washington—consider schools to be a basic and fundamental concern of taxpayers.

Clearly, the more government involves itself in education, the less kids learn. Government's response to this realization has been to centralize more authority over the schools—away from local control, to state and federal levels.

The tragic part of this charade is that most Americans still don't catch on. They themselves have been so miseducated by a barrage of government propaganda in the schools and corporate establishment press over the last thirty years that they eagerly buy into the false prescriptions of the public education quacks.

I daresay even most of those reading this book—an unusually bright and informed group—have subjected their own kids to government schools that are intentionally denying kids the basic education they need to govern themselves responsibly.

Just one in four high-school seniors could identify two ways the U.S. system of government prevents the exercise of "absolute arbitrary power," according to the 1998 results of the National Assessment of Educational Progress evaluation. The same survey found that one-third of high-school seniors had no idea the Bill of Rights was written to limit the power of the federal government.

In a 1998 poll conducted by the National Constitution Center, not one in fifty American teenagers could identify James Madison as the father of the U.S. Constitution. The same poll found more than half could not name the three branches of the federal government.

It's not easy writing about the insanity rampant in America's government schools. It's a little overwhelming. Take the 1999 story of the seventh grader in Ponder, Texas. Christopher Beamon and his English class were asked by their teacher, Amanda Henry, to write a Halloween essay—a work of fantasy, a fictional short story. It was understood by teacher and class alike that scary material would be incorporated into the writing exercise.

Beamon wrote a spooky one, all right. A school essay on getting high? Waiting for a drug connection? Turning to inhaling deadly Freon gas as a stimulant when the drugs didn't show up? Then unloading a shotgun and a 9mm on hapless students and the very teacher who assigned the essay?

Yup. That's about the size of it. But here's where it gets interesting. The teacher loved it. According to reports in the Associated Press and elsewhere, though later denied by school officials, Mrs. Henry gave young Christopher an A—100 percent perfectamundo. He even got extra credit for reading the illiterate essay, chock-full of vulgarity and grammar and spelling errors, to the entire class.

In other words, Beamon was honored for his work—until some of the parents of students named as victims in the essay complained to Principal Chance Allen. Allen did what any red-blooded government bureaucrat would do in such a situation—he called the cops. The next thing you know, young Chris was arrested for his prize work and jailed in a juvenile detention center for five days.

After reading Beamon's essay, the following thought comes to me: *If anyone should be jailed in this case, it should be the school officials who failed so miserably to teach this kid how to write.*

What's amazing about the controversy over the essay is the intolerance of fantasy violence—clearly mimicking the kind of stuff this kid watches on MTV—and the apparent lack of concern by all with the seventh grader's knowledge and preoccupation with getting high.

None of this craziness took place in a major urban school district where confusion and gun fears reign supreme. This all happened in a farm town of about five hundred, forty miles from Dallas.

How can anyone, let alone a thirteen-year-old kid working on a school assignment, be locked up for writing anything in the land of the First Amendment?

How can a school district reconcile giving a kid an A on an assignment and then calling the cops on him for the same work?

I tend to think of this kid as a victim of government schools. But at the same time, what scares me about him is not his knowledge of weapons, but his hip-hop, urban-beat, gangster self-image that I suspect is all too common among today's young teens.

What were the failing essays like?

I could go on and on. But this incident is not really as unusual in its official absurdity as it seems. Every week now, there are news reports of seven-year-olds being suspended for bringing nail clippers to school, government officials trying to determine which kids might be mass murderers through standardized tests, kids expelled for drawing pictures of guns, etc.

It would be funny if it weren't so frightening. This is scarier than any Halloween story I have ever heard. What has happened to our concept of education? What has happened to our concept of civil rights? What has happened to our concept of common sense?

The inmates are truly running this asylum. Government schools are not only breeding illiteracy among students, but are obviously subsidizing it among teachers and administrators.

Parents, if you don't think your government school is just as scandalous and shameful in its standards and values, you are living in a dream world.

The answer is not to be found in national standards, more government intervention, and higher taxes for more public education. The only solution to this abysmal performance is for responsible parents everywhere to pull their kids out of government schools—now!

You may think your school is doing a pretty good job—relatively speaking. Relatively speaking doesn't say very much. Your kids deserve better. They deserve real education, not the kind of socialization and indoctrination that government offers.

The best solution seems, to most parents, to be wholly impractical. That's homeschooling.

"Oh, I don't have time," parents say. "My husband and I both work. Anyway, I don't think I would be an effective teacher for my kids. I've forgotten so much that I learned in school."

Hey, I've got news for you. You're in a much better position to give your kids an education than the government is. You love them. You care about them. You understand their individual needs. No matter what you think of yourself, you're just as smart as those government school teachers.

The next-best solution is to find a good private school that teaches kids biblical truth.

All knowledge and all truth begin with the Scriptures. Oh, I know what you're saying out there: "Farah, get over it! Where do you get this stuff? The Bible is just a collection of old myths."

If that's what you believe, if that's what you'd like your kids to believe, I feel sorry for you. But for those of you who understand what I'm saying, it's time to put your beliefs into practice.

None of us will be suitable for the task of self-governance without this kind of guidance. George Washington, the father of our country, understood this principle.

"Of all the dispositions and habits which lead to political prosperity, religion and morality are indispensable supports," he wrote. Continuing, he said:

In vain would that man claim the tribute of Patriotism, who should labor to subvert these great Pillars of human happiness, these firmest props of the duties of Men and citizens. The mere Politician, equally with the pious man ought to respect and to cherish them. A volume could not trace all their connections with private and public felicity. Let it simply be asked where is the security for property, for reputation, for life, if the sense of religious obligation desert the oaths, which are the instruments of investigation in Courts of Justice? And let us with caution indulge the supposition, that morality can be maintained without religion. Whatever may be conceded to the influence of refined education on minds of peculiar structure, reason and experience both forbid us to expect the National morality can prevail in exclusion of religious principle.

He added, "'Tis substantially true, that virtue or morality is a necessary spring of popular government. The rule indeed extends with more or less force to every species of free Government. Who that is a sincere friend to it, can look with indifference upon attempts to shake the foundation of the fabric?"

In other words, it's a hopeless task to teach kids the fundamentals of civics and history without the spiritual and moral context. Do you think the government will ever be able to do that? Will you allow your kids to settle for less?

The people who control and run government schools—or what some people mistakenly call "public schools"—are working very hard to ensure they have no competition, especially from pesky parents who actually think they know what's best for their kids.

"Home-schooling programs cannot provide the student with a comprehensive education experience," the National Education Association, the biggest teacher union in the country, states. Reaffirmed in July 2000 at the labor union's annual convention, the statement was originally adopted and published in 1988.

The resolution, which totals less than 150 words, also states: "Home schooling should be limited to the children of the immediate family, with all expenses being borne by the parents/guardians. Instruction should be by persons who are licensed by the appropriate state education licensure agency, and a curriculum approved by the state department of education should be used."

"The association also believes that home-schooled students should not participate in any extracurricular activities in the public schools," the resolution concludes.

Now, isn't that interesting? How's that for arrogance? How's that for ignoring reality? How's that for throwing stones while living in a glass house?

So, homeschooling cannot provide the student with a comprehensive education experience, huh? Why is it that every study shows homeschoolers far outperforming those miseducated in government schools? (Calling them "public schools" is misleading because most "private schools" in this country are open to the public. The difference is that what we call "public schools" are actually institutions controlled by the state—and increasingly by Washington.)

According to a 1998 study conducted by Dr. Lawrence M. Rudner, a quantitative analysis expert, students who are educated at home have consistently scored far above the national average in standardized tests. Rudner's qualifications and credentials in establishment education circles make him an unlikely champion of homeschooling. He has served as a university professor, a branch chief in the U.S. Department of Education, and a classroom teacher. For the past twelve years, he has been the director of the ERIC Clearinghouse on Assessment and

Evaluation. ERIC is an information service sponsored by the National Library of Education—a branch of the Education Department. His two children attend public school.

His study included a total of 20,760 students in 11,930 families—seven times as many homeschooling families as any previous study of its kind—which provided demographic questionnaires and achievement tests. And unlike earlier studies, families chose to participate before they knew their children's test scores.

In other words, this was a scientific study. And what were the results?

"In every subject and at every grade level of the ITBS and TAP batteries, home school students scored significantly higher than their public and private school counterparts," the *Washington Post* reported.

According to the study, home-schooled children score in the 82nd to 92nd percentile ranking for reading and up to the 85th percentile in math. About 25 percent of all homeschooled students are enrolled one or more grades above their age levels, with the achievement gap widening as students progress. By the eighth grade, the average homeschooled student performs four grade levels above the national average.

Meanwhile, need I recite the dismal performance record of government schools over the last thirty years? Declining test scores, rampant violence, high-school graduates who can't read?

It's no wonder the NEA is so worried about homeschooling. It may be the biggest and best threat to the government education establishment. While most voucher and school-choice plans could easily be co-opted by the state, it's hard to imagine how government could ever corrupt homeschooling, short of regulating it or outlawing it. And that's just what the state's partner in education crime—the NEA—is trying to do.

The NEA, which has demonstrated high marks only for dumbing down an entire generation of government school students, now wants to license parents to teach their own kids.

Of course, the group objects to homeschooling because it cannot possibly offer a comprehensive educational experience for kids. But at the same time, the NEA wants to make sure it doesn't—so don't get any ideas about trying to sneak your homeschooled kid into a government school extracurricular program, even if your tax dollars did pay for it.

Unbelievable.

Worse, because of the big campaign contributions the NEA provides, many politicians are running a protection racket for the powerful union. The NEA is running a protection racket for its employees. But more than that, the NEA is spearheading the drive for total government control over all education. The reason it does so is because government empowers the NEA. This is a union that has special privileges no other labor guild has ever enjoyed—including nonprofit status for an organization that actively promotes, endorses, and funds the candidacies of partisan political campaigns.

This is truly an extremist organization—one that would, if it could, change America's character in ways that would make it scarcely recognizable to freedom-loving people.

And that's why homeschoolers are its biggest enemy, its most-feared threat, and its most worthy adversary.

Maybe you think I'm overstating the case when I tell you that government schools are intentionally dumbing down students. Maybe you can't think of any motivation for such an insidious goal.

I believe there is an objective—and it is a very logical one for people determined to create more dependence on government, to maintain a constituency of perpetual serfdom. That's what I think. There is nothing compassionate about miseducating students, about not teaching kids to read, write, and speak clearly. That's just what advocates of the government education monopoly do.

What do government bureaucracies love more than anything else? Customers. Dependents. Constituents. That's what government schools create—more people for government to take care of, more reasons to redistribute wealth, more reasons to empower government.

I suspect most Americans actually believe they're smarter than their parents and grandparents. That shows just how dumb most Americans really are.

The fact is that the average Joe was much more well-educated a hundred years ago—before government secured its virtual monopoly grip on schooling in America.

I could take the time to present a body of empirical and historical evidence to prove that statement. But let me make the case today with just one anecdotal submission. The following is an 1895 eighth-grade final exam from Salina, Kansas. It was taken from the original document on file at the Smoky Valley Genealogical Society and Library in Salina, Kansas, and reprinted by the *Salina Journal:*

GRAMMAR
(Time: One Hour)

1. Give nine rules for the use of Capital Letters.

2. Name the Parts of Speech and define those that have no modifications.

3. Define Verse, Stanza and Paragraph.

4. What are the Principal Parts of a verb? Give Principal Parts of *do, lie, lay and run.*

5. Define Case, Illustrate each Case.

6. What is Punctuation? Give rules for principal marks of Punctuation.

7–10. Write a composition of about 150 words and show therein that you understand the practical use of the rules of grammar.

ARITHMETIC
(Time: 1.25 Hours)

1. Name and define the Fundamental Rules of Arithmetic.

2. A wagon box is 2 ft. deep, 10 ft. long, and 3 ft. wide. How many bushels of wheat will it hold?

3. If a load of wheat weighs 3,942 lbs., what is it worth at 50 cts. per bu., deducting 1,050 lbs. for tare?

4. District No. 33 has a valuation of $35,000. What is the necessary levy to carry on a school seven months at $50 per month, and have $104 for incidentals?

5. Find cost of 6,720 lbs. coal at $6.00 per ton.

6. Find the interest of $512.60 for 8 months and 18 days at 7 percent.

7. What is the cost of 40 boards 12 inches wide and 16 ft. long at $.20 per inch?

8. Find bank discount on $300 for 90 days (no grace) at 10 percent.

9. What is the cost of a square farm at $15 per acre, the distance around which is 640 rods?

10. Write a Bank Check, a Promissory Note, and a Receipt.

U.S. HISTORY
(Time: 45 Minutes)

1. Give the epochs into which U.S. History is divided.

2. Give an account of the discovery of America by Columbus.

3. Relate the causes and results of the Revolutionary War.

4. Show the territorial growth of the United States.

5. Tell what you can of the history of Kansas.

6. Describe three of the most prominent battles of the Rebellion.

7. Who were the following: Morse, Whitney, Fulton, Bell, Lincoln, Penn, and Howe?

8. Name events connected with the following dates: 1607, 1620, 1800, 1849, and 1865?

ORTHOGRAPHY

(Time: One Hour)

1. What is meant by the following: Alphabet, phonetic orthography, etymology, syllabication?

2. What are elementary sounds? How classified?

3. What are the following, and give examples of each: Trigraph, subvocals, diphthong, cognate letters, linguals?

4. Give four substitutes for caret 'u.'

5. Give two rules for spelling words with final 'e.' Name two exceptions under each rule.

6. Give two uses of silent letters in spelling. Illustrate each.

7. Define the following prefixes and use in connection with a word: Bi, dis, mis, pre, semi, post, non, inter, mono, super.

8. Mark diacritically and divide into syllables the following, and name the sign that indicates the sound: Card, ball, mercy, sir, odd, cell, rise, blood, fare.

9. Use the following correctly in sentences: Cite, site, sight, fane, fain, feign, vane, vain, vein, raze, raise, rays.

10. Write 10 words frequently mispronounced and indicate pronunciation by use of diacritical marks and by syllabication.

GEOGRAPHY

(Time: One Hour)

1. What is climate? Upon what does climate depend?

2. How do you account for the extremes of climate in Kansas?

3. Of what use are rivers? Of what use is the ocean?

4. Describe the mountains of N.A.

5. Name and describe the following: Monrovia, Odessa, Denver, Manitoba, Hecla, Yukon, St. Helena, Juan Fernández, Aspinwall and Orinoco.

6. Name and locate the principal trade centers of the U.S.

7. Name all the republics of Europe and give capital of each.

8. Why is the Atlantic Coast colder than the Pacific in the same latitude?

9. Describe the process by which the water of the ocean returns to the sources of rivers.

10. Describe the movements of the earth. Give inclination of the earth.

Can you imagine today's eighth graders handling such a test? Can you imagine high-school graduates or even college graduates passing such an exam? How many college professors can you imagine mastering it?

How far have we come as a nation of free, moral, educated, self-governing individuals? So far that those adjectives have been rendered meaningless by a government education system specifically designed to create dependency rather than foster self-reliance.

Have you been in any urban public schools lately? They are not education facilities; they are detention camps. They are not places of learning; they are militarized day-care centers. They are not schools at all, but social conditioning facilities designed to produce slaves to the state. Whatever learning does take place does so by accident or in spite of the obstacles.

Rebellion usually begins where conditions are most severe. This is why in Communist strategy, activists are urged to bring on repression in free societies. Repression is a catalyst for change of all kinds—including, sometimes, change for the worst.

What's happening in government schools today is nothing short of child abuse. That's why so many parents are opting out—by the millions. When millions more join them—without fanfare, without protest marches, without letters explaining their decision, without the involvement of politicians—the revolution will have begun in earnest.

The whole system will collapse—not just the education system, but the system of centralization of authority, the system of forced dependency, the system of government control over our lives.

Every day Americans ask me what they can do to fight back—to take America back. The most important step we can take—the single most dramatic action—is also the most important to your family, to your children. Get them out of the government indoctrination centers. Take responsibility for educating your kids; don't leave it to the state.

It's an important first step. This is how the revolution can be won without firing a shot. This is our Lexington and Concord. This is our Declaration of Independence. Get your kids out of the clutches of these monsters. Do it now. Do it for them. Do it for your country.

★ 10 ★

CRIME AND PUNISHMENT

Laws that forbid the carrying of arms . . . disarm only those who are neither inclined nor determined to commit crimes . . . Such laws make things worse for the assaulted and better for the assailants; they serve rather to encourage than to prevent homicides, for an unarmed man may be attacked with greater confidence than an armed man.

—THOMAS JEFFERSON

THE PHONE RANG IN THE DISTRICT OF COLUMBIA'S BUSY 911 emergency hot line center as it does hundreds, sometimes thousands, of times a day.

A burglary was in progress at a private home. The police department employee who handled this particular call assured the caller assistance was on its way. But instead of getting the high-priority code a "crime in progress" is supposed to get, the dispatcher assigned a lower priority to the call.

When police officers finally arrived at the scene of the burglary, they failed to make a thorough check of the building and left without discovering the two burglars, who by this time had raped a four-year-old girl and forced her mother to commit sodomy.

The victims' neighbors, two women who lived upstairs, made a second 911 call, again receiving assurance that help was on the way. No help ever arrived. For the next fourteen hours, the intruders held all the occupants of the building captive, including the two women who lived upstairs; they were all raped, robbed, beaten, and subjected to numerous sexual attacks.

It's a tragic and true story—one you need to understand if you are concerned about freedom, self-protection, crime, and punishment in America today.

Why? Because, despite all this abuse and ineptitude, the court in the nation's capital later issued an important ruling in this case. The victims received no settlement from the government. No one in government was punished. And the court found that neither the assurance of assistance nor the fact that the police had begun to act suggested in any way that the city or police officers were liable for failure to respond properly.

"[T]he desire for condemnation cannot satisfy the need for a special relationship out of which a duty to specific persons arises," ruled the court in *Warren v. District of Columbia*. Because the complaint did not allege a relationship "beyond that found in general police responses to crimes," this court affirmed the dismissal of the complaint for failure to state a claim.

In other words, the police aren't there to protect average citizens.

I doubt most Americans realize their governments—local, state, and federal—are not there to protect them. Even after September 11, 2001, it has not registered with many. Government sees its role as cleaning up after the attack—whether it is an attack on a home, a random shooting, or a full-scale terrorist attack against large numbers of civilians.

Sometimes it happens. There are brave police officers who put their lives on the line for strangers. They are to be applauded. But most police work occurs after the fact. Most responses are postvictimization.

So in a free society, who is primarily responsible for protecting you? You are.

Is this a shocker? It shouldn't be. Government can't and won't take responsibility for protecting you. It would love to take responsibility for feeding you, providing you with prescription drugs, making sure you have adequate day care for your children, educating your children, and a thousand other jobs that have no constitutional basis in America. But it will not assume the critical job of protecting you. You are on your own there.

The government doesn't advertise this shortcoming. It doesn't announce it. It seldom admits it. But it is a brutal reality. The government can't protect you from hijacked airliners. It can't protect you from incoming missiles. It can't protect you from common criminals who seek to rob and kill you and your family.

Government can only react to these attacks.

Think about it.

The next time a politician suggests tougher government gun control is needed to fight violent crime, look around and count his armed bodyguards.

While the calls for disarming average, taxpaying Americans have increased in recent years, the government expenditures on armed security for politicians and bureaucrats has increased dramatically.

Is what's good for the goose not so good for the gander?

If politicians believe we're safer with fewer guns around, why is it that they are increasing the number of armed federal police? Why is it that they are cordoning off government buildings? Why is it that they are beefing up armed guards in government buildings?

Easy. They know that they need guns to protect themselves against real threats and as a deterrent against criminals, terrorists, and nuts.

Do the American people deserve any less? Do those who actually pay for the security of their government officials deserve to be disarmed and left helpless before the threats they face in their own neighborhoods?

All this raises the question: What is the purpose of antigun laws? What is the real agenda? Simple. It's government empowerment. Notice who are the prime agitators for more gun control. They are the same people who promote more government control over all facets of our lives—education, health care, child care, and the economy. They seek, ultimately, the complete disarmament of the civilian population of the United States. They will never stop whining about gun violence until they pry the guns from our cold, dead fingers. Why? The government-control advocates want us to place our fate in the hands of the state. Our lives, our fortunes, and our sacred honor should be entrusted to the police for protection, they say. Truly, though, safety and security can only be achieved when individuals take responsibility for themselves.

I have all the respect in the world for police officers, but, quite candidly, most are not really there "to protect and to serve." They are there to take reports and maintain files. And even that mission is overwhelming to them at times.

All the police power and all the laws in the world will not make you, your family, and your neighbors safe. The only thing that can offer you some protection is a well-regulated trigger finger and a good aim.

Why can't Americans see the obvious? Why don't they understand what our founders saw so clearly more than two hundred years ago? The government, no matter how benign it may seem, is not your friend. It does not have your best interests in mind. Left to its own devices and unchecked by a vigilant population, governments will always seek more and more power.

Most Americans have grown to trust their government to protect them and their rights.

This is why Americans are flirting with a loss of all freedom.

If you wonder what a total government power monopoly will be like, all you need to do is examine the reaction by government schools to the armed attacks on students in recent years.

Remember, government schools in all fifty states long ago banned firearms. Not even teachers or administrators would think of keeping a loaded gun on campus to protect themselves and their student charges. Thus, those attending government schools are sitting ducks for anyone who wants to go out in an ignominious blaze of gore.

The shooting and bombing attacks have only increased. So what's the next step?

School districts all over America are increasingly treating all students like criminals. School systems are banning book bags, lunch boxes— even coats and jackets—from school premises for fear they might be used to conceal weapons.

What's going on here? Has America gone mad? Is this overreaction or collective insanity?

I'm afraid it's neither. Instead, it's the predictable eventuality when government is given the authority, tacitly or otherwise, to be the sole provider—or, as we've already seen in this chapter, the sole non-provider—of our safety, security, and liberty. That's where we're headed in America. The government schools are already there.

So what's the solution?

Of course, I could tell you what you've heard before from other authors, other commentators. I could urge you to write to your congressmen. I could say you should join some of the good organizations promoting self-defense and gun rights. But I have a more direct solution—a more radical idea.

My advice is to go out and buy guns—buy more than you think you need. Buy ammunition—lots of it. Train yourselves in the use of firearms. Become an expert. Go target shooting. Teach your children to use guns responsibly. You will be doing more to deter crime and preserve freedom than any letter-writing campaign could ever muster. Actions speak louder than words. And so do guns.

If the 10 or 20 percent of Americans who understand what I am saying do this, it will put an end to all the talk about gun control. The debate will be over. We will have won a major victory. Actions speak louder than words. This is one more step in taking America back. Buy guns for yourself—and buy them for the people you love.

On Christmas Day, 2001, I sent my mother-in-law packing.

You think I'm mean? You think I'm a bad son-in-law? You think I have no feelings? You think I'm heartless?

Maybe you don't understand.

I didn't kick her out of the house. I love my mother-in-law. She's a great lady—a good grandmother.

What I mean is this: Elizabeth and I bought her a gun for Christmas.

Now, for some of you out there, this news may be even more shocking than kicking her out or knocking her down a flight of stairs.

But let me explain why giving someone you love a gun is the ultimate demonstration of concern and compassion.

Firearms are great equalizers. A little old lady with a little training and a gun is more than a match for some criminal miscreant or predator—no matter how big or scary he might be.

It's because I want my mother-in-law to live out her natural life safe from such potential attackers that I gave her a gun. Even more than that, I want her to feel safe and secure when neither I nor my better-armed wife are around to defend hearth and home.

She often watches my kids too. I can't imagine allowing an unarmed granny to watch our eighteen-month-old. Unthinkable. Ridiculous. Repugnant.

Now, some of you are going to squeal in disbelief, "You mean you allow guns around your children?"

You bet. And as soon as they are physically able to do so, we teach them how to shoot too. Guns can be great equalizers even for little people.

I can't believe how squeamish Americans have become about guns. It's time for a total reeducation on the matter of firearms.

It wasn't that long ago that kids carried their firearms to school so they could belong to gun clubs and participate in competitive shooting. Now schools are gun-free zones. Are kids any safer in schools? No way. They are at far greater risk.

The most dangerous place in America is a gun-free zone, because only law-abiding people will respect the rules that govern it. Therefore, the only armed people, by definition, will be criminals.

It's so easy to understand. Why are Americans so confused?

Look at merry old England. Well, it's not so merry anymore. Since banning firearms, the murder rate with guns has skyrocketed. Once again, when you outlaw guns, only outlaws have guns.

We can't let that happen in America—especially after the September 11 wake-up call.

Americans, I believe, have been under the mistaken impression that their government would protect them from foreign and domestic enemies of all kinds. Now we know that isn't true.

What the government does is respond to the heinous acts of foreign and domestic enemies. It doesn't prevent their attacks. It merely counterattacks—sometimes, maybe, if it feels like it, if the evidence is solid enough to warrant it, if the victim is alive to testify in court, if, if, if . . .

Only a well-armed citizenry is an effective countermeasure to deter crime and other threats on our life and liberty. There's no substitute. None. Zilch.

And it's most important to arm the weak, the defenseless, the vulnerable, the likely victims. Most guys I know like guns. Most women don't. Guess what? Women need them more.

For some of you, I'm preaching to the choir. You know more about guns than I do. You're angry because the government is making it more difficult to get the guns you want and feel you need. You sense it's only a matter of time before Big Brother comes knocking on your door to collect them.

Well, don't sit back and wait for it to happen. And don't count on the effectiveness of writing letters of protest to your gutless member of Congress. Instead, take action. Arm yourselves while you can. Give the gun industry its biggest boost ever. Stimulate the firearms economy. Start an arms buildup right here in America. And watch the crime rate drop before your eyes.

There's a side benefit too. The more Americans who are packing heat, the more difficult and unpopular it will be for the government to grab the guns.

And don't forget your mother-in-law.

Buy guns? Buy ammo? I know some readers are going to react with concern to this advice. Some Christians, in particular, are going to suggest this prescription to fight crime and preserve freedom is unbiblical, unscriptural, and ungodly.

Wrong.

The Bible couldn't be clearer on the right—even the duty—we have as believers to self-defense.

Let's start in the Old Testament.

"If a thief be found breaking up, and be smitten that he die, there shall no blood be shed for him," we are told in Exodus 22:2. The next verse says, "If the sun be risen upon him, there shall be blood shed for him; for he should make full restitution; if he have nothing, then he shall be sold for his theft."

In other words, it was perfectly OK to kill a thief breaking into your house. That's the ultimate expression of self-defense. It doesn't matter whether the thief is threatening your life or not. You have the right to protect your home, your family, and your property, the Bible says.

The Israelites were expected to have their own personal weapons. Every man would be summoned to arms when the nation confronted an enemy. They didn't send in the Marines. The people defended themselves. In 1 Samuel 25:13 we read: "And David said unto his men, Gird ye on every man his sword. And they girded on every man his sword; and David also girded on his sword: and there went up after David about four hundred men; and two hundred abode by the stuff." Every man had a sword and every man picked it up when it was required.

Judges 5:8 reminds us of what happens to a foolish nation that chooses to disarm: "They chose new gods; then was war in the gates: was there a shield or spear seen among forty thousand in Israel?"

The answer to the rhetorical question is clear: No. The people had rebelled against God and put away their weapons of self-defense.

"Blessed be the LORD my strength, which teacheth my hands to war, and my fingers to fight," David writes in Psalm 144:1.

Clearly, this is not a pacifist God we serve. It's a God who teaches our hands to war and our fingers to fight. Over and over again throughout the Old Testament, His people are commanded to fight with the best weapons available to them at that time.

And what were those weapons? Swords.

They didn't have firearms, but they had side arms. In fact, in the

New Testament, Jesus commanded His disciples to buy them and strap them on. Don't believe me? Check it out.

Luke 22:36: "Then said he unto them, But now, he that hath a purse, let him take it, and likewise his scrip: and he that hath no sword, let him sell his garment, and buy one."

I know, I know. You biblically literate skeptics are going to cite Matthew 26—how Jesus responded when Peter used his sword to cut off the ear of a servant of the high priest: "Then said Jesus unto him, Put up again thy sword into his place: for all they that take the sword shall perish with the sword. Thinkest thou that I cannot now pray to my Father, and he shall presently give me more than twelve legions of angels? But how then shall the scriptures be fulfilled, that thus it must be?" (vv. 52–54).

Read those verses in context and they support my position. Jesus told Peter he would be committing suicide to choose a fight in this situation—as well as undermining God's plan to allow Jesus' death on the cross and resurrection.

Jesus told Peter to put his sword in its place—at his side. He didn't say throw it away. After all, He had just ordered the disciples to arm themselves. The reason for arms was obviously to protect the lives of the disciples, not the life of the Son of God. What Jesus was saying was, "Peter, this is not the right time for a fight."

In the context of America's current battle—as we make plans to rebuild after the devastation of September 11 and defend ourselves at the same time—we should recall Nehemiah, who rebuilt the walls of Jerusalem.

"They which builded on the wall, and they that bare burdens, with those that laded, every one with one of his hands wrought in the work, and with the other hand held a weapon," we're told in Nehemiah 4:17–18. "For the builders, every one had his sword girded by his side, and so builded."

Do we really believe we are wiser than the great men who founded this country? Do we really believe they enshrined in the Second Amendment the right to bear arms because they wanted to protect the rights of hunters, as some politicians today tell us? Are we ready, in spite of all we know about the basic nature and character of government, to entrust our basic freedoms to the state and its armed agents?

For those who are, let me make a suggestion. Why don't you set an example for the rest of us and print up signs for your homes that say, "This is a firearm-free zone"? This would represent a real service to the country. We can experiment to see if their thesis is correct. Does a reduction in firearms translate to a reduction in violence? This will be the test case.

I say, go for it. After all, what do you have to worry about? You've got the police and the government to protect you.

The gun-control crowd argues that the Second Amendment has become an anachronism in the modern age because we have the government to protect us from enemies and the police force to protect us from criminals.

As someone who trusts government about as much as I trust criminals, I never had much use for that argument. And while I generally think most local policemen are good people, as I've shown, they honestly just can't be relied upon to protect you.

There is only one logical conclusion you can draw from the way federal gun laws are passed and enforced. Gun-control regulations, as we understand them today, are not really meant to deter criminals from getting their hands on guns. In fact, it serves the gun grabbers' interests when criminals get guns and use them. Every violent crime makes their cries for more government control of firearms palatable to the American people.

The government-control advocates want us to place our fate in the hands of the state. Our lives, our fortunes, and our sacred honor should be entrusted to the police for protection, they say. I agree with the founders: Safety and security can only be achieved when individuals take responsibility for themselves.

And that's the real reason Americans need to rearm as a primary step in taking America back.

Yes, guns deter crime. Yes, the Constitution guarantees our right to do so. Yes, the Bible justifies self-defense. But the only way—the only way—we can ever hope to keep our government accountable to the people is for the people to be well armed.

The founders understood this well—all of them:

George Washington: "Firearms stand next in importance to the Constitution itself. They are the American people's liberty teeth and keystone under independence."

Thomas Jefferson: "And what country can preserve its liberties, if its rulers are not warned from time to time, that this people preserve the spirit of resis-tance? Let them take arms . . . The tree of liberty must be refreshed from time to time with the blood of patriots and tyrants."

Richard Henry Lee: "To preserve liberty it is essential that the whole body of the people always possess arms and be taught alike, especially when young, how to use them."

Alexander Hamilton: "If the representatives of the people betray their constituents, there is no recourse left but in the exertion of that original right of self-defense which is paramount to all forms of positive govern-ment" (Federalist 28). And: "The best we can hope for concerning the people at large is that they be properly armed" (Federalist 46).

While more guns in the hands of responsible Americans will certainly translate to more government accountability and less crime, such a trend will not eliminate crime. And that's why we also need to take a new look at the way we punish lawbreakers in America today.

Are more prisons, tougher sentencing, and mandatory jail time the answers to the crime problem we have in America today? I admit, I once thought so.

Not anymore. Not by a long shot.

Just twenty-five years ago, there were fewer than 250,000 men and women in American prisons. Today there are more than 2 million.

Has crime fallen? No, not really.

You will hear some statistics that suggest the trend is down, especially for property and violent crimes. Even so, any progress achieved by the temporary lockup of offenders is overshadowed by the consequences of what prison does to inmates.

Prisons are crime schools.

The unfortunate truth is that almost all prisoners are going to be released someday. And under the current criminal university system, they are better crooks, better killers, and better equipped not to get caught when they are released.

The recidivism rate is around 70 percent. Do the math: When those 2 million prisoners hit the streets again, 1.4 million of them are not only going to commit new crimes, but they are going to get caught for their crimes.

Let's face it: We all know that most crime *does* pay—at least in the short term. Most criminals do not get caught the first or even second time they commit an offense. That means our prisons today are merely breeding grounds for millions of new offenses yet to be perpetrated on the public.

"The huge prison bulge may temporarily slow down crime, as it apparently has, but as offenders are released, the number of new crimes can be expected to skyrocket," explains Charles Colson in *Justice That Restores.*

It's similar to what we do with the federal deficit—pass along the real costs of our excesses and mistakes to our children. This approach just doesn't work in the long term.

What is the answer, then?

Colson suggests, and I agree, that we need to examine the real root causes of crime. It's not about poverty, as some suggest. It's about morality—a sense of right and wrong. That's a concept we have retreated from in America in recent times.

We are reaping the whirlwind of cultural decay.

When you see the American Civil Liberties Union and other groups attacking the posting of the Ten Commandments in classrooms in this country, you are witnessing a dramatic example of that attack on moral absolutes and a headlong rush toward moral relativism.

There are indeed absolutes, and we all know it. It's wrong to kill, and it's wrong to steal. The basis for that understanding is the Ten Commandments. Like it or not, that's the source for our common consensus on right and wrong. It's time to stop pretending that you can have morality apart from such common denominators that serve as the very basis for our societal compact.

But the problem with criminal justice in America today is even more specific than that.

Why do we lock people up for crimes? To punish them. Nobody truly believes it is a matter of rehabilitation anymore.

Surely there are people so depraved, so corrupt, so dangerous to society that they need to be removed from society—people like the fictional Hannibal Lecter. In a just society, those people should be executed. Period. End of story. What purpose does it serve to incarcerate them where they are a potential danger to guards and other prisoners, and always a risk to escape?

For the rest—and the overwhelming majority of prisoners—it's time to consider a completely new approach. And there are some excellent experimental programs under way that show promising results.

I'm talking about what Colson calls "restorative justice." I'm talking about restitution.

When you are victimized in some way, what good does it do to lock up the perpetrator where he continues to burden society with the heavy costs of incarceration in prisons with television sets, three squares a day, air-conditioning, workout rooms, etc.?

I think the criminal should be compelled by the state, working in partnership with organizations like Colson's Justice Fellowship, to make restitution to their victims. To the best of their ability, they need to make their victims whole. That may mean working for them. That may mean paying them off. That may mean a host of different things depending on circumstances.

But the amazing side impact of such programs is the restorative impact they have on the criminal. And that means there will not only be real justice served, but there will be fewer victims in the future.

This is real compassion. It's something government can't do. But people can. And if we want to take America back, we need to start thinking outside the box—and outside the prison walls.

★ 11 ★

Anglo-Saxon civilization has taught the individual to protect his own rights; American civilization will teach him to respect the rights of others.

—WILLIAM JENNINGS BRYAN

I believe each individual is naturally entitled to do as he pleases with himself and the fruit of his labor, so far as it in no wise interferes with any other man's rights.

—ABRAHAM LINCOLN

REMEMBER REV. MARTIN LUTHER KING'S "I HAVE A Dream" speech?

I say to you today, my friends, that in spite of the difficulties and frustrations of the moment, I still have a dream. It is a dream deeply rooted in the American dream.

I have a dream that one day this nation will rise up and live out the true meaning of its creed: "We hold these truths to be self-evident: that all men are created equal."

I have a dream that one day on the red hills of Georgia the sons of former slaves and the sons of former slave owners will be able to sit down together at a table of brotherhood.

I have a dream that one day even the state of Mississippi, a desert state, sweltering with the heat of injustice and oppression, will be transformed into an oasis of freedom and justice.

I have a dream that my four children will one day live in a nation where they will not be judged by the color of their skin but by the content of their character.

I have a dream today.

That's what he said at the foot of the Lincoln Memorial on August 28, 1963.

I have a dream too.

I have a dream that America will return to its heritage of freedom.

But before that dream is realized, we've got to stop miseducating kids at every turn. What do I mean? Take what your kids are learning today about Martin Luther King and the principles of American freedom.

Just take a look at the garbage being produced to commemorate King's birthday.

"Civil rights are the freedoms and rights that a person has as a member of a community, state, or nation," writes Kathy Wilmore, in an article in *Scholastic* magazine titled "Civil Rights: How Far Have We Come?" She continues, "In the U.S., these rights are guaranteed to all citizens by the Constitution and acts of Congress."

No ma'am, that is not true. Civil rights, America's founders taught us so well, are God-given, inalienable rights. They don't descend from government. They are not given out through acts of Congress. They are not even granted by our Constitution. They cannot be invented by man. They are inherent, universal, permanent.

This is such a foundational point of understanding American civic life, history, and government that it cannot be a simple mistake by an educational publisher. This is deliberate brainwashing—an example of the dumbing-down process we hear so much about in government schools. What these institutions produce is not educated students so much as spare parts for a giant statist-corporate matrix called America.

As if to underline her point, she adds, "Since the 1960s, many laws have been passed to guarantee civil rights to all Americans. But the struggle continues. Today, not only blacks, but many other groups—including women, Hispanics, Asian-Americans, people with disabilities, homosexuals, the homeless and other minorities—are waging civil-rights campaigns."

If *Scholastic* is correct about rights simply being extended by legislative decree, then rights can be taken away as easily as they are bestowed. Those are not rights, folks. Those are privileges.

Notice the subtle way the struggle by blacks is equated with agitation by "the homeless" and homosexuals. This is Marxist Indoctrination 101. I know; I used to use such techniques myself. But now it is thoroughly permeating not just academia, but elementary schools and private educational companies that sell their products to the government educational monopoly.

"Most people agree that decent housing is a basic right," she goes on. "Yet millions of Americans live in substandard housing—or have no housing at all. They live that way because they cannot afford better—or are kept out of better housing by discrimination (unfair treatment)."

Oh, really? That strikes me as a pretty strong statement to make without citing any evidence. "Most people agree that decent housing is a basic right." Hmm. I would challenge that supposition. Even in America's advanced case of intellectual, moral, and cultural decay, I don't believe a majority would now say that decent housing is a basic right. At least I hope not.

But even if some poll showed that the statement might be technically true, I have to add a big "So what?" Who cares what people think about rights? It doesn't matter. Once again, rights—true rights—descend from God and cannot be given to man nor taken away by anyone else.

We also learn from *Scholastic* materials that King got his ideas for peaceful resistance from two sources—Mahatma Gandhi and Henry David Thoreau. Gee, you know, I don't deny that those folks were influences on King, but to ignore King's inspiration from the Bible is ludicrous.

After all, it was Jesus who taught us—Gandhi and Thoreau included—about loving your enemy and "turning the other cheek."

Ah, but then, of course, you have the old sticky wicket of religion in the classroom. Better to simply ignore reality—the truth that Martin Luther King was a Christian minister. I have a feeling that not many kids in government school will hear this part of Martin Luther King's "I Have a Dream" speech:

I have a dream today.

I have a dream that one day every valley shall be exalted, every hill and mountain shall be made low, the rough places will be made plain, and the crooked places will be made straight, and the glory of the Lord shall be revealed, and all flesh shall see it together.

This is our hope. This is the faith with which I return to the South. With this faith we will be able to hew out of the mountain of despair a stone of hope. With this faith we will be able to transform the jangling discords of our nation into a beautiful symphony of brotherhood. With this faith we will be able to work together, to pray together, to struggle together, to go to jail together, to stand up for freedom together, knowing that we will be free one day.

This will be the day when all of God's children will be able to sing with a new meaning, "My country, 'tis of thee, sweet land of liberty, of thee I sing. Land where my fathers died, land of the Pilgrims' pride, from every mountainside, let freedom ring."

And if America is to be a great nation this must become true. So let freedom ring from the prodigious hilltops of New Hampshire. Let freedom ring from the mighty mountains of New York. Let freedom ring from the heightening Alleghenies of Pennsylvania!

Let freedom ring from the snowcapped Rockies of Colorado!

Let freedom ring from the curvaceous peaks of California!

But not only that; let freedom ring from Stone Mountain of Georgia!

Let freedom ring from Lookout Mountain of Tennessee!

Let freedom ring from every hill and every molehill of Mississippi. From every mountainside, let freedom ring.

When we let freedom ring, when we let it ring from every village and every hamlet, from every state and every city, we will be able to speed up that day when all of God's children, black men and white men, Jews and Gentiles, Protestants and Catholics, will be able to join hands and sing in the words of the old Negro spiritual, "Free at last! free at last! Thank God Almighty, we are free at last!"

Freedom, freedom, freedom, freedom. That was the King message. Martin Luther King talked a lot more about freedom than he did rights. He was clear on where true freedom and rights came from. That distinction has been obliterated in today's teaching about him.

Why? Because freedom cannot be controlled by government. Government would prefer to define the limits of your freedom by arbitrarily creating new "rights" and disabusing us of the notion that rights are God's inalienable gifts to all humanity.

Today, the self-proclaimed inheritors of King's movement no longer talk much about freedom. They seldom mention from where our rights descend. Instead, they tell us that what made America great is *diversity.*

You hear that often these days. You hear it in government schools. You hear it from our politicians. You hear it from the talking-head pundits on TV. It's stated as a matter of fact—an article of faith.

This isn't what made America great. It's not what made life in America great for me or for my grandparents. What made America the place to be for my immigrant grandparents was something much different from diversity. It was something called freedom. And today, in our misguided, headlong rush to embrace phony diversity, we're giving up that precious gift of freedom.

Let's examine this myth of diversity. If, in fact, people are basically the same—regardless of race or ethnic background—why would this kind of diversity mean anything to a society? Think about it. The diversity proponents are the very people emphasizing differences between the races. They see the world made up of groups, not individuals.

The proof that they believe some of those groups are inherently inferior to others is that they create different standards of achievement and expectations for them, as in "affirmative action."

They actively oppose laws designed to treat all people equally regardless of skin color and ethnic background, because they are truly racist to the core, and, even more important, because the conflict they create in the process helps empower them.

You see, governments don't liberate people. People liberate themselves from government. That's the way it has always been and that's the way it will always be until the good Lord comes again.

The diversity crowd cloaks its true agenda behind nice-sounding words and lofty objectives. What it is really about is rigid, authoritarian conformity—totally intolerant of any ideas that threaten the movement and its hideously disguised plans for empowerment.

Here's the key to real freedom: Human beings don't have group rights. They have individual rights. The diversity proponents want to change that. They rise to power by identifying groups for "favored" treatment. We've got some goodies for you, they say. And enough people buy it to change a society's fundamental precept that it is individuals, not groups of people, who are bestowed by their Creator with the right to pursue life, liberty, and happiness.

Fundamentally, these people don't like America. But instead of founding their own country as our founders did, they are trying to steal your America—your birthright.

Let me give you an example of what I'm saying: Representative Jesse L. Jackson Jr., the heir apparent to the Rainbow Throne, says the U.S. Constitution is "inadequate" to handle the needs of African-Americans. He called the document "unfinished business" for blacks.

Jackson made his comments in the context of the presidential election quagmire of 2000 and made it clear that his contempt for the Constitution is one of the reasons he supported Vice President Al Gore so enthusiastically.

"Some of us are with Al Gore because he would give us a broader interpretative [sic] group of constitutional judges who would look at the Constitution and see women as women and see African-Americans as full citizens and see people as people . . . equal protection under the law," he said, quoted in the *Chicago Defender*. "The common denominator is that the Constitution of the U.S. is inadequate of [sic] handling the needs of our community. Our basic fundamental rights that should be inalienable are not so inalienable and not so self-evident."

He continued: "It doesn't mean that we are any less American because we acknowledge that the Constitution from our perspective is inadequate. We are more American because we recognize that the Constitution represents unfinished business."

Exactly what does Junior think the Constitution is lacking?

Well, he has filed two constitutional amendments to correct what he says is the inadequacy of the Constitution to meet the needs of blacks, other minorities, and poor people.

"Health care ought to be your human right, not your Democratic or Republican Party right," he explains.

There you have it, folks. A candid admission from a U.S. congressman, who, last time I checked, is still required to swear an oath to uphold the Constitution to serve in the House of Representatives, telling it like it is—forget the Constitution.

It's not his Constitution, he suggests. It's a Constitution for rich white folks of the male persuasion.

Did you hear even one of his Democratic or Republican colleagues in the House call for censure or even offer a mild rebuke of Jackson for his assault on the Constitution? I haven't—nor do I expect to hear any such criticisms. That's the real problem—most of his colleagues have no respect for the Constitution either. At least Jackson admits it.

Jackson and his ilk do not seek equal protection under the law— because that is precisely what the Constitution requires. What they truly seek is unequal protection under the law—special favors under the law. In fact, they seek to use the law only as a tool for achieving their own political and economic empowerment.

For once a member of the Jackson clan has it exactly right. The U.S. Constitution paves the way only to liberty, self-reliance, and self-governance. To achieve their agenda, they must put the final nails in the coffin of the most remarkable freedom document ever crafted.

Let me show you how this "group rights" philosophy actually destroys freedom. One of the catchphrases of this movement is "equal pay for equal work." It sounds good. How can one argue with such a simple, fair-minded concept?

Women, proponents say, earn seventy-three cents for every dollar earned by a man. That's not fair. How do the "group rights" proponents aim to fix this injustice? They will toughen enforcement of laws already on the books that ban wage discrimination based on gender. In other words, paying one equally qualified person less for the same job because she's a woman is already illegal. Anyone who is a victim of such discrimination has plenty of recourse right now under the law. The next step is to empower the government to find discrimination not in actual individual cases, but through statistical analysis. Bottom line? More federal wage-and-price cops.

The mere fact that women in a certain company are paid less than men will become a prima facie case of wage discrimination—and harsh penalties will be imposed on employers.

But there are some problems with the statistics. The numbers cited by "equal pay for equal work" activists in no way suggest that the wage disparity between men and women is for equal work, just equal amounts of work. But even that is probably not accurate, since many jobs held by men (management and sales, to name two) aren't paid on an hourly basis. The hours expected of people in those positions is far greater than forty.

The truth is there are many social and cultural issues that contribute to the fact that women earn less than men.

Men are not paid equally for equal work. Women are not paid equally for equal work. In fact, I bet it would be difficult to find two people anywhere in the world who are being paid exactly equal amounts for exactly equal work.

Now, don't get me wrong. I don't think women should be paid less because they are women. In fact, I'll tell you a secret. I have hired women and paid them more than the men they replaced—sometimes far more. I've also paid them less.

As a chief executive officer of an Internet company, I can tell you that hiring decisions and salary negotiations are very subjective matters. They are also among the most personal matters in which we as Americans engage. And it is none of the government's business.

This equal pay idea goes well beyond misguided egalitarianism. It illustrates where such naively ignoble concepts lead. It starts when the government decides, as a principle, that "a person's gender should not be a consideration in the setting of his or her salary." That sounds good. I might even decide to practice it as an employer for business and ethical reasons. But it leads to exactly the opposite principle being enforced by the government. Now the government wants to force companies to consider the employee's gender a factor.

But there are many other factors that go into the setting of salaries. Does experience mean anything? Does productivity? Does the marketplace?

And notice that it's OK with the government to pay men less than women. This is a crooked one-way street of inequality. This is payback time—reparations time, affirmative action time, quota time, whatever you want to call it.

By the way, the language of this debate is beginning to change. Often the proponents of this "equal pay" idea now talk about "equal pay for comparable work." By default, the activists have acknowledged just what I am saying—that there is no such thing as "equal work." Now the argument is for equal pay for "comparable" work.

As always with people who want to undermine constitutional government for their own empowerment, they are misstating a statistic for the purpose of turning it into a societal problem that probably doesn't exist at all, and, to the extent it might exist, can never be solved through the kind of government action they propose anyway.

Why do they do this?

It's an example of the oldest political trick in the book—divide and conquer. They divide the population into competing constituency groups—the rich against the poor, minorities against whites, women against men, young against old. This strategy permits them to empower themselves as the great moral arbiters in virtually every facet of our lives.

Think about it. Let's say my lawn needs mowing and I'm too tired after working eighty hours a week just to pay the taxes I owe to the government. There's a guy on the corner with a sign that says, "Need work." The days are over when I can go up to that man and offer him a crisp ten-dollar bill to mow my lawn.

After all, there's the Social Security tax that must be withheld. Legally, I should have to issue him a 1099 form to file with the Internal Revenue Service, and I am required to report that payment to the IRS. I must make certain I am not in violation of state and federal regulations on minimum wage requirements. I must ascertain that he is a legal resident of the United States. And on and on I could go.

Why? Because the government inserts itself between people in even the most basic, mutually beneficial transactions. And the so-called equal-pay laws are just one more way to ensure the government gets its cut of any commercial action that takes place in America. It's a power play. It's not about compassion for women; it's about restricting our most basic and cherished freedoms of association.

What do we do about this? How do we respond? How do we fight back?

Americans must educate themselves about their heritage of freedom. Some of us must become articulate enough to take on the activists—to challenge their terms, to reframe the debate, to remind the nation what makes us unique and great.

Read the Constitution. Study it. Read the Declaration of Independence. Study the other founding documents. Understand the American concept of freedom—a truly revolutionary idea. And fight for it. Don't be intimidated by the conventional wisdom of the day. Be smart. Be right. Know your facts. Know the truth. And it will set you free.

Do you want your children to be free? Or do you want them to grow up living in a world of political correctness—where the government decides what's "fair" and what "equality" is?

You've got to rise up, America. You've got to stop taking the abuse of your inalienable rights. Understand what's at stake—life, liberty, and the pursuit of happiness. The threat you are facing is much graver than the threat our founders faced.

You've got to rebel—not just lobby. You've got to say no—not just choose the lesser of two evils. You've got to stop participating in the madness—not continue to subsidize it. You've got to fight—not just complain.

That's how we will take America back.

★ 12 ★

ENTER THE INTERNATIONALISTS

The great rule of conduct for us, in regard to foreign nations, is in extending our commercial relations to have with them as little political connections as possible . . . It is our true policy to steer clear of permanent alliances with any portion of the foreign world.

—GEORGE WASHINGTON

EARLIER I PROVIDED EXAMPLES OF JUST A FEW OF THE ways government squanders your hard-earned tax dollars on wasteful, unconstitutional, pork-barrel spending projects that only serve to empower those doling out the loot.

Those wealth-redistribution programs, however, all took place because of specific votes in the House of Representatives and the U.S. Senate and were approved by the president of the United States. But did you know tax dollars are frequently—routinely—given away by the *billions* without so much as a vote in Congress?

Here's an example: Partly as a favor to President Clinton, worried in his first term about a crash in the Mexican economy that could jeopardize the appearance of the NAFTA "partnership," Bear Stearns's chief economist Wayne Angell, a former Fed governor, came up with an idea for a massive transfer of wealth from America to south of the border. Angell said the $40 billion peso bailout could come from the obscure Exchange Stabilization Fund.

But as Bob Woodward points out in *Maestro*, Angell had another motivation besides helping Clinton. His investment bank had underwritten many endangered securities in Mexico.

Senator Robert Bennett, R-Utah, served as the intermediary who took the idea to Fed Chairman Alan Greenspan and Treasury Secretary Robert Rubin. Both of those men were wary of the potential for Congress to second-guess the plan and embarrass them in public by exposing the blatantly unconstitutional scheme.

"What happens if you do it and Congress is silent?" Bennett reportedly asked Greenspan.

Greenspan had to admit that would work. If there was a guarantee of congressional silence, he would go along with the plan.

Bennett proceeded to go to Senate Majority Leader Bob Dole to ascertain if he would block all efforts to bring this wealth-transfer scheme to a vote. He got the promise. Then Bennett went to House Speaker Newt Gingrich, who ran the idea up the flagpole with then Texas Governor George W. Bush. The future president liked the idea, so Gingrich gave his approval.

And that's an example of how your tax dollars are given away to support the narrow self-interests of a few elite bankers without any accountability. That was once called "taxation without representation." That was once the basis for the greatest war of independence ever waged. That was once the battle cry of a hardy band of freedom-loving people. Now it happens every day. Americans yawn. They take it for granted. Or, more often than not, they live in blissful ignorance.

Abuses like this occur because of corrupt, unconstitutional institutions such as the Fed, the International Monetary Fund, and the World Bank. They all serve the banking elite—not the people of the United States—even though we largely fund them.

If this bugs you as much as it does me, you need to shout about it. You need to say "Not with *my* money!" You need to rise up in righteous indignation. You need to realize you are being robbed blind. This is not even legalized theft—this is merely theft by deception and by overwhelming force.

Most of all, you've got to stand up tall against the march toward global political and economic unions that afford the American people no accountability, that recognize no inalienable rights, and that create supranational governments that can only lead to tyranny on a worldwide scale.

From my point of view, globalism represents government encroachment's final frontier. Having proved itself totally incapable of guarding individual rights, personal freedom, and national sovereignty even under the best of circumstances, as in the United States, globalists intend to take their social engineering and wealth-transfer experiments worldwide.

By definition it is un-American to submit sovereign citizens of the United States to laws, treaties, regulations, and foreign authorities to which they have no accountability. Last time I checked, we Americans don't elect any representatives to the United Nations, the World Trade Organization, the Millennium Assembly and Summit, the G8 (Group Of Eight), the Organization of Economic Cooperation and Development, the Bank of International Settlements, the World Bank, the International Monetary Fund, the European Union, the North American Free Trade Association, the Westminster UNA, the One World Trust, the Commission for Global Governance, the Royal Commonwealth Society, the World Federalists Association, the Earth Council, the State of the World Forum, or any other multinational body.

In his famous farewell address, George Washington warned the nation about such foreign entanglements—though I doubt he could even imagine how naively Americans would fall into their trap.

World government is a profoundly un-American idea. And worse yet, the global conspirators—and there is simply no other way to describe them—are planning to hand over control of our lives and livelihoods to worldwide authorities who would like nothing better than to see America knocked down a notch or two, all in the name of "leveling the playing field."

They'll use any means necessary to get us there—including lying about and hyping crises, both real and imagined, such as global warming, AIDS, and overpopulation. They are all just means to an end.

And what is that end? It's the further centralization and consolidation of power—this time on a worldwide scale. That's what all these multinational treaties are really about. They are moving us toward global governance—away from the constitutional principles and foundations of the American republic, away from limited government, away from checks and balances.

Many Americans still buy the lie that only a worldwide body such as the United Nations can really move the world closer to peace. The track record of the international body hardly supports such a notion.

Remember the horror of the Rwanda tribal genocide in 1994? In a few months, as many as one million people were killed. Who was the United Nations secretary-general back then? It was an Egyptian by the name of Boutros Boutros-Ghali. He and the U.N. were criticized for standing by while the slaughter took place.

But less known is the fact that Boutros-Ghali actually played a leading role in supplying weapons to the Hutu regime that carried out the campaign of genocide against the Tutsi tribe during his tenure as top executive at the U.N.

As minister of foreign affairs in Egypt, Boutros-Ghali facilitated an arms deal in 1990, which was to result in $26 million of mortar bombs, rocket launchers, grenades, and ammunition being flown from Cairo to Rwanda. The arms were used by Hutus in attacks that led to up to a million deaths. Boutros-Ghali, who was in charge at the U.N. when it turned its back on the killings in 1994, admits his role in approving an initial $5.8 million arms deal in 1990, which led to Egypt supplying arms to Rwanda until 1992. He says he approved it because it was his job as foreign minister to sell weapons for Egypt.

Did you catch that? He was just doing his job—just following orders. Sound familiar?

As reported in Linda Melvern's *A People Betrayed*, the weapons were smuggled into Rwanda disguised as relief material. At the time there was an international outcry at human rights abuses by the Hutu government as thousands of Tutsi were massacred. Asked about the wisdom of an arms deal at such a sensitive time, Boutros-Ghali said he did not think that a "few thousand guns would have changed the situation." His contacts with the Hutu regime have never been investigated. Why? Who's going to investigate the head of the U.N.? To whom is he accountable? To whom is the U.N. accountable?

And that's really the problem with these international government bodies.

The U.N. is not just, as many Americans suspect, a group of incompetent busybodies. It is instead a global criminal enterprise determined to shift power away from individuals and sovereign nation-states to a small band of unaccountable international elites.

Here are some of the ways the U.N. has trod on U.S. sovereignty in recent years:

- The U.N. has designated American geographic wonders from Niagara Falls to the Grand Canyon to Lake Tahoe as "World Heritage Areas," and instructed the citizens of the United States on how we should behave around these "international" treasures.

- The United States Army has, in the case of Bosnia and elsewhere, been drafted into service to the U.N. Michael New, a serviceman who swore allegiance to the Constitution and the United States when he signed up for duty, refused to don U.N. colors, and serve under U.N. command. He was court-martialed and dishonorably discharged for his principled and logical stand.

- The U.N. sent an investigator from Senegal into the United States to look into capital punishment as a human rights abuse based on a Geneva-based commission's report about an increase in U.S. executions, racism in the use of the death penalty, and other complaints.

Now do you understand why people are getting nervous when they see U.N. vehicles patrolling American streets or when they hear about

U.N. officials investigating environmental abuses alongside employees of the Environmental Protection Agency? Kind of makes you wonder where all this is leading, doesn't it?

Earlier I discussed the growing threat to our inalienable right to self-defense posed by the federal government. The United Nations is also getting into the gun-control business, suggesting private owner-ship of firearms is a dangerous and outdated idea and that, for the safety and well-being of all concerned, only governments should be entrusted with such authority.

The real truth is that only an armed and vigilant citizenry stands between freedom and, as we saw in Rwanda, genocide. Government, on the other hand, is the only power on earth capable of the kind of mass annihilation for which the twentieth century is notorious.

"About 170 million men, women and children have been shot, beaten, tortured, knifed, burned, starved, frozen, crushed, or worked to death; buried alive, drowned, hanged, bombed, or killed in any other of the myriad ways governments have inflicted death on unarmed, helpless citizens and foreigners" in this century, explains University of Hawaii professor R. J. Rummel, who studied the phe-nomenon of genocide for his landmark book, *Death by Government.*

No other century has come close to the carnage of the twentieth, he writes.

"It is as though our species has been devastated by a modern Black Plague," he says. But this plague is a "plague of power."

Rummel's estimates of the death toll, remember, are based on doc-umentary evidence, in most cases provided by governments them-selves. Thus, the actual number is probably much higher—perhaps as high as 360 million, he says.

Without question, socialist regimes, those that monopolize power in government, have been by far the deadliest culprits. Since 1949, for instance, one in every twenty Chinese citizens has been murdered, starved, or killed by their own government. More than 50 million civilians wiped out in "peacetime."

And it is the unarmed civilian population that always pays the highest price. During this century, four civilians died for every soldier killed fighting in wars.

The Soviet government was the second-biggest butcher regime, not only in the last one hundred years, but throughout history. Many of the civilian deaths, such as those who died of starvation in Joseph Stalin's Ukrainian terror famine, were murdered by government-dictated quotas. In sheer numbers, the Chinese and Soviet holocausts made Hitler's look trifling by a comparison.

More recently, from 1975 through 1979, more than two million Cambodians, or 31 percent of the population, were destroyed by a government edict inspired by utopian pipe dreams. That belief in power as a tool of changing societies, combined with government's superior firepower, is the big difference. That's been standard operating procedure this century, says Rummel.

Whether it was Hitler's Germany or Stalin's Soviet Union or Mao's China, the first step toward civilian "pacification"—and ultimately mass murder—is the strict control of private gun ownership. Just a handful of guns in the Warsaw ghettoes kept the Nazis at bay for many months.

To get a picture of just how many people have been exterminated by government, imagine this: If you lined up all these victims and marched them at three miles per hour, twenty-four hours a day, seven days a week, with three feet between them, Rummel figures it would take five years and nine months for the grisly parade to end. Unfortunately, it would start right up again with the latest atrocities in Bosnia, Somalia, Sudan, Rwanda, and inevitably wherever the next government-sponsored genocide occurs.

Ask yourself, Would this—could this—have happened if the citizenry of these countries had the right to bear arms as we in the United States have had for the last two hundred years? In every case, there is a common denominator—raw government power and a disarmed civilian populace.

Are we really ready to consider worldwide control and regulation of private gun ownership? If so, just imagine what the body count will be like in the twenty-first century.

Virtually no one in the United States government is standing up for our sovereignty and our individual rights by demanding that we withdraw from the U.N., and most important of all, stop funding this madness with U.S. taxpayer dollars.

In 1999, $1.4 billion extorted from the American people by the federal government was transferred to the U.N. But that's just the tip of the iceberg of what the U.S. "contributes." According to figures cited by U.S. Senator Jesse Helms in his January 20, 2000, speech to the U.N., the American taxpayers also spent an additional $8,779,000,000 from the United States' military budget to support various U.N. resolutions and peacekeeping operations around the world.

How would I characterize such an "investment"? Irresponsible, foolish, theft, and counterproductive, if the goal is peace and freedom in the world.

Just say things like this today and you need to be prepared for a tsunami of name-calling and ridicule from the elite media—those who get paid to parrot what passes as "conventional wisdom."

The very first word they will hurl at you is *Isolationist.*

I've been called a lot worse. I'm not sure I'm an isolationist, and I don't like anyone labeling me, but America could stand a dose of isolationism in the twenty-first century. Do you know that even before the war on terrorism began in late 2001 the U.S. had troops in more than a hundred foreign countries?

Why?

What's the worst crisis facing the world today? Famine? Ethnic wars? Terrorism? Middle East tension? Chinese expansionism?

Those are all serious problems, to be sure. But, I think one could make the case that the greatest evil being perpetrated on the grandest scale is the systematic persecution of Christians.

Christians are the most persecuted group in the world today. Eleven countries now practice systematic persecution of Christians, says author Nina Shea in her book, *In the Lion's Den.* They are China, Pakistan, Laos, North Korea, Vietnam, Cuba, Saudi Arabia, Sudan, Egypt, Nigeria, and

Uzbekistan. These eleven nations—and others that practice a more random brand of persecution—are dominated by one of two belief systems, Communism or militant Islam.

Between 60 million and 100 million Christians face persecution in China today. Think about the size of that group. That's a church bigger than its counterpart in the United States—and it's underground, illegal, cruelly oppressed.

Islamic Sudan has abducted or killed more than 1 million of its own people in a jihad against non-Muslims. Young Christian boys are held captive, forced to convert to Islam, and then sold as slaves. There are even reports of crucifixions of Christians in Sudan.

When we think of Christian persecution, our thoughts turn to Rome and the Coliseum lions. Yet what's happening today is far worse—both in terms of numbers and brutality. Never before in the history of the world have so many Christians been persecuted for their beliefs—an estimated 200 to 250 million Christians are at risk.

"We are not talking about mere discrimination," says Shea, director of the Puebla Program on Religious Freedom, "but real persecution—torture, enslavement, rape, imprisonment, forcible separation of children from parents."

I have seen videos smuggled out of China showing the activities and precautions of what they call the "home church" movement. When I had heard this term before, I assumed people met in small groups. Yet this video shows groups of hundreds, perhaps thousands, meeting in heavily wooded areas and caves. Emotions run high. You wouldn't mistake one of these meetings with an American church service. There's dancing and singing and clapping and tears and laughter unlike anything I have ever witnessed before.

And it's no wonder they are so energized. In China, thousands have been sentenced to "reeducation camps" for simply attending one of these services or a Bible study meeting.

I could only imagine that the words of Jesus, recorded in the gospel of John, must have been ringing in their ears:

If the world hate you, ye know that it hated me before it hated you. If ye were of the world, the world would love his own: but because ye are not of the world, but I have chosen you out of the world, therefore the world hateth you. Remember the word that I said unto you, The servant is not greater than his lord. If they have persecuted me, they will also persecute you; if they have kept my saying, they will keep yours also. But all these things will they do unto you for my name's sake, because they know not him that sent me. If I had not come and spoken unto them, they had not had sin: but now they have no cloak for their sin. He that hateth me hateth my Father also. If I had not done among them the works which none other man did, they had not had sin: but now have they both seen and hated both me and my Father. (15:18–24)

Have you heard any scathing U.N. reports about Christian persecution? Of course not. The U.N. hides it, obscures it, downplays it. The U.N. is complicit in this slaughter.

Proponents of and apologists for the U.N. and the dozens of other global acronyms increasingly threatening our freedom like to say that we live in an "interdependent" world today. They don't really believe our country represents a unique experiment in freedom and independence.

The trouble with "interdependence" is that it is still dependence. Look it up. It is not in America's best interests to be dependent on any other country, any other leader, any other people—even if they are dependent upon us as well. It is for this ideal of independence that our revolutionary forebears fought and died in the fields of Lexington and Concord and at the battles of Bunker Hill and Trenton.

Are concepts like independence and sovereignty now outdated? Have they outgrown their usefulness? Have they been scrapped in favor of some other vision without so much as a national debate?

There are people, many of them in Washington, who would like America locked in a world of interdependent relationships. They'd like to take us where Europe is today and where it's going tomorrow. That is not a pretty picture. The European Union, GATT, NAFTA,

NATO, the United Nations, and other supranational alliances mean less accountability, less responsive government, more centralization of authority, and less freedom.

Isolationist? You don't scare me by throwing the *"I"* word around. A little isolationism would be healthy for America. Less foreign aid, fewer military engagements and "peacekeeping" missions, fewer treaties, and more focus on our own national security interests would be a good thing—a great thing.

Think about it. We can't fix the whole world. The best thing we can do as a nation is to provide an example—to be that "shining city on a hill." We can also take care of our own. I don't mean with welfare, food stamps, and other government dependence programs—but with liberty and prosperity.

We can't have liberty and prosperity without national security. That's why I would take all the money we throw away playing nurse-maid to the Third World and redirect it to a strategic national defense program and civil defense to protect the American people from attack. We need to be able to defend this country from incoming ballistic missiles. We need to be able to protect citizens from terrorism and the threat of weapons of mass destruction being driven here by truck. We have no such defense today.

Nada.

There is a role for U.S. foreign intervention. There is a time and place for military involvements. But, on those rare occasions we, as a nation, must be certain that those commitments are in our vital national interests.

That's why I say America could use a dose of isolationism. We must do a better job picking our spots, making good foreign policy choices, forming temporary alliances when it suits us, but avoiding the kind of permanent foreign entanglements about which George Washington warned us.

Washington was a truly great man and leader. As great as the other founders were, not one was his peer. He was the unparalleled military leader who led the war of independence, and he was the glue that united the states in some contentious days before the Constitution was drafted and ratified.

We not only owe this man our respect and veneration, but we also owe it to ourselves to heed his final warnings to the nation. I think he has a message for us today, as we are about to embark on a war without a mission—a war that seems to have more to do with "domestic affairs" and political motivations than any clear national security objective.

"The Government sometimes participates in the national propensity, and adopts through passion what reason would reject," he warned in his farewell address. "At other times, it makes the animosity of the Nation subservient to projects of hostility instigated by pride, ambition and other sinister and pernicious motives. The peace often, sometimes perhaps the Liberty, of Nations has been the victim."

Washington also understood the concept that peace is best kept through strength. In his first presidential address, he stated it cogently: "To be prepared for war, is one of the most effectual means of preserving peace."

Today, many of our elected leaders believe in wishful thinking that stands this sound principle on its head. Their lowest priority is a military prepared for war. They overcommit defense forces in so-called "peacekeeping" missions—really global police work. They cut and slash only at military budgets in phony and shortsighted efforts to reduce deficits. They destroy the morale of soldiers by using the armed forces for experiments in social engineering. And they forget the meaning of defense—confusing it with offense and the ability to project force around the world.

"Against the insidious wiles of foreign influence (I conjure you to believe me, fellow citizens), the jealousy of a free people ought to be constantly awake; since history and experience prove that foreign influence is one of the most baneful foes of Republican Government," Washington prophesied. "Real Patriots, who may resist the intrigues of the favorite (nation), are liable to become suspected and odious; while its tools and dupes usurp the applause and confidence of the people, to surrender their interests."

Does this sound familiar, my fellow Americans? Do you know any "tools" or "dupes" of foreign interest in high places in twenty-first-century America?

Washington believed in "temporary alliances for extraordinary emergencies." He would not have looked favorably upon post–Cold War NATO, the United Nations, the World Trade Organization, Most Favored Nation status, or the North American Free Trade Agreement. I guarantee it.

"The Great rule of conduct for us, in regard to foreign Nations is in extending our commercial relations to have with them as little political connection as possible," he said. "So far as we have already formed engagements let them be fulfilled, with perfect good faith. Here let us stop."

Washington made that pronouncement only three years before he died. It wasn't self-interest that led him to make such a warning. It was experience. It was wisdom. It was integrity. Does anybody remember integrity?

We'll have to reacquaint ourselves with the concept if we hope to take America back.

WHAT IS SELF-GOVERNMENT?

We have staked the whole future of American civilization, not upon the power of government, far from it. We have staked the future of all our political institutions upon the capacity of mankind for self-government, upon the capacity of each and all of us to govern ourselves, to control ourselves, to sustain ourselves according to the Ten Commandments.

—JAMES MADISON

BULLETIN: AMERICAN PEOPLE RULED UNFIT TO GOVERN.

WASHINGTON—In a historic decision with major implications for the future of U.S. participatory democracy, the Supreme Court ruled 8-1 Monday that the American people are unfit to govern.

The controversial decision, the first of its kind in the 210-year history of the U.S. representative government, was, according to Justice David Souter, "a response to the clear, demonstrable incompetence and indifference of the current U.S. citizenry in matters concerning the operation of this nation's government."

As a result of the ruling, the American people will no longer retain the power to choose their own federal, state and local officials or vote on matters of concern to the public.

That was an April 18, 1999, report from *The Onion*, a satirical online publication (www.TheOnion.com). They say humor only works if there is a grain of truth in it. In this case, there may be more than a grain of truth.

America is indeed losing its ability to govern itself.

I was on the Fox News Channel's *Hannity & Colmes* program defending a July 4 column I wrote on why Americans are less free today than they were in 1776.

Eleanor Clift was there, along with Alan Colmes, to try to set me straight.

I launched into an explanation of how we have lost the founders' concept of self-government today—and that without it the Declaration of Independence and the best Constitution ever devised by man aren't enough to keep our nation free. I suggested that nine out of ten Americans don't even know what self-government means.

Clift jumped in and began her attack.

"Well, I would point to local communities, and I think people are more interested in taking a role in how they are governed in their immediate neighborhoods and cities and towns than they are in how the central government is operating," she said.

To which I replied: "I think that Eleanor just betrayed that she's one of the nine out of ten Americans who do not understand what self-government is. It's not about local government, state government, or central government. It's about governing ourselves as individuals, being accountable to God, having a morality that guides us in our actions."

Self-government. Even Eleanor Clift of *Newsweek* doesn't know what it means.

The War of Independence was fought 226 years ago principally over the issues of sovereignty and self-government.

These are two concepts that have been obliterated from the debate today. The war was fought so that we in America would have the ability and right to govern ourselves as individuals and that our individual states would have sovereignty with little interference from London, Washington, or anywhere else.

Do we have that today?

Let's just talk about taxes—since that was such an important issue in the War of Independence.

Just like in 1776, we have taxation without meaningful representation. In 1994, for instance, Americans elected Republicans to both houses of Congress for the first time in decades because they promised, among other things, to scrap the tax code. They lied. Let's not mince words. They failed to live up to their "Contract with America," and Americans have not had an opportunity to express their rage against the unconstitutional income tax since.

Today the tax code is every bit as complicated and confiscatory as it was before 1994, if not more so.

We've been living with an unconstitutional income tax in this country now for nearly ninety years. Why is it unconstitutional? Because it is in direct violation of the Fourth Amendment: "The right of the people to be secure in their persons, houses, papers, and effects, against unreasonable searches and seizures, shall not be violated, and no warrants shall issue, but upon probable cause, supported by oath or affirmation, and particularly describing the place to be searched, and the persons or things to be seized."

You just try invoking your Fourth Amendment rights to the IRS when it comes to make a claim on you.

Is there any doubt that Americans don't like the income tax? Do you think most Americans would trade it or scrap it if they could? If we had real representation, would it still be around? Of course not. Americans have no choice. The game is rigged—just as it was rigged against the colonials.

Washington is every bit as unaccountable to the people as the British Crown was. But Washington has more power, more force, more ability to coerce.

That's why we have far less liberty than our founding fathers had.

In 1776, Americans were much freer to govern themselves, and the states had less accountability to the Crown than they do today to Washington. Today, Washington is God. The Ninth Circuit ruling on the Pledge of Allegiance is a perfect example. What Washington says goes. Who cares about common sense and the Constitution?

Washington dictates policies to the states and local governments and holds individuals accountable to thousands of unconstitutional laws—and declares perfectly constitutional laws invalid with a stroke of the pen. That's not the way our country was designed.

Does America have the courage to recover the freedom it has lost in the last two hundred years? That is the question.

Too many Americans, in my opinion, are overly concerned with safety and security, and not nearly enough are concerned about freedom and liberty.

That's the trap that government always uses to lure power away from the self-governing individual. Self-government is what George Washington and his barefoot men sacrificed for in the snows at Valley Forge. It wasn't simply a matter of independence from the crown of England. It was a war fought so that free men could govern themselves.

The founding fathers believed in the principle that the nation that governs least governs best. They believed that an educated people, a moral people, a courageous people would be up to the task of running their own lives.

And that's why the colonists fought.

It was a much bigger and more profound concept than national sovereignty.

Are we willing to fight today? Thomas Jefferson believed we as a people needed to mix it up, even spill a little blood, every so often to maintain our liberty. Are Americans willing to fight for our freedom?

I am. And this book is written as a rallying cry for others out there to join me.

Freedom isn't about prescription drug plans dictated by Washington. Freedom isn't about more laws. Freedom isn't about a false security promised by your federal government. Freedom isn't about being numbered from cradle to grave. Freedom isn't about having your wealth confiscated by government before you even cash your paycheck. Freedom isn't about the government miseducating your child. Freedom isn't about United Nations peacekeeping missions. Freedom isn't about more cops on the beat.

Freedom, ultimately, is about the liberation of the individual to run his or her own life with minimal interference from government. Period. End of story.

Are we prepared in America to renew the dream of self-government?

It's time for renewal in America—spiritual renewal.

Freedom is unknowable and unachievable apart from the promises of God. So, maybe the best place to start this Second American Revolution is just where George Washington started his—down on his knees. It's time to pray for America's moral and spiritual restoration.

It's America's last, best hope for preserving and rediscovering true freedom.

I understand this is not a very "PC" statement to make. "Politically correct"—what a concept. Maybe it's time for a new slogan—a new shorthand, bumper-sticker expression that can help bind people together around a common vision and belief system. A long time ago, now, some misguided soul got the notion that "politically correct," or "PC," would do that.

But "political correctness" quickly deteriorated into a means of marginalizing people and groups that didn't subscribe to fashionable cause, such as statism and the denial of individual rights and personal responsibility.

Webster's definition of "political correctness" is "conforming or adhering to what is regarded as orthodox liberal opinion on matters of sexuality, race, etc.: usually used disparagingly to connote dogmatism, excessive sensitivity to minority causes."

That's actually pretty good for modern *Webster's*. I might change "orthodox" to "unorthodox," but I don't want to quibble.

In any case, "political correctness" has become a curse to those who first employed it. That's because it was, from the start, an attempt to intimidate those with different ideas from expressing them. It was an effort to coerce, to stifle debate. Debate itself became "politically incorrect" to the neofascists who invented "political correctness."

The truth is that good people often disagree about politics. Politics is, after all, merely a vehicle to achieve certain objectives in government. Or, to resort once more to modern *Webster's*, "the science and art of political government; political science; political affairs; the conducting of or participation in political affairs, often as a profession; political methods, tactics, etc.; sometimes, specifically, crafty or unprincipled methods; political opinions, principles, or party connections; factional scheming for power and status within a group."

Again, not bad. And it illustrates the point I'm trying to make in an effort to popularize a new "PC" expression. Who cares if someone is "politically correct" or "politically incorrect"? Politics, for my money, is a rather lowly ambition.

The real issue ought not to be whether our leaders, would-be leaders, friends, neighbors, etc. are "politically correct." It ought to be a concern as to whether they are "principly correct." Now, don't split hairs with me and tell me that "principly" is not a word. Give me a break. I know that. That's part of the beauty of this expression. It should be a word. And it will be.

You see, I think we're missing the boat if we judge our politicians on this particular stand or that one. The real issue ought to be whether they are principled. Are they motivated by fundamental truth, freedom, the rule of law, and morality?

From where does their sense of right and wrong descend? Is it from man? Or is it from a higher authority? Is their morality evolving, or is there an immutable standard by which they live and make decisions? Are they subject to superficial temptations like money, fame, favorable polls, and good press? Or do they stand up for their beliefs no matter what?

That's what I mean by "principly correct." Do you like it a little better now? Is it growing on you?

Under this new expression and definition, I'm proud to be PC. And you should be too.

Forget politics. Politics is a game. It's the means to an end—any end, good or evil. But principles are principles. Unprincipled people, like so many politicians in Washington today, have no business in power. Their motivations are not truth, freedom, the rule of law, and morality. They have no respect for any of those things.

They are thus very "principly incorrect." And those who would impose their wills upon us in the guise of "political correctness" are all "principly incorrect."

I don't usually like labels. In fact, I detest them. But I can get behind this idea of "principly correct." I would proudly wear that label. How about you?

Let me give you an example of "principly incorrect." Every election cycle, the politicians start courting "the God vote."

I don't mean by this that they are studying the Holy Scriptures to determine God's will for man. I don't mean they are prayerfully contemplating their own ambitions and motives to determine if they are pure. I don't mean they are prostrating themselves before the Supreme Being in an effort to judge their own worthiness for high office.

No, I don't mean any of these things. What I mean is that they are arrogantly, presumptuously, and shamelessly courting the political support of the tens of millions of Americans who not only believe in God, but worship Him regularly as the Alpha and Omega.

It gets pretty silly out there. While most of the candidates like to talk about their own faith, stage photo ops in churches, and be seen carrying Bibles, they're also eager to show how "grown up" they are about such matters.

In the 2000 presidential contest, for instance, Vice President Al Gore was asked if it would bother him should an atheist become president of the United States.

Maybe you missed it. Here's what he said: "No, it would not. I think that it would depend on who the person was, of course. But do I believe that someone can have an understanding of our Constitution [and] a true spirit of tolerance without affirming a particular and specialized belief in God? Yes, I do. I think that is incumbent upon anyone who affirms a respect for tolerance."

Gobbledygook? Yes. But it's the kind of psychobabble that demands analysis.

There's so much here in this short statement—and yet so little.

Gore asserts it is possible that an atheist can understand the Constitution. Has anyone ever suggested otherwise? There's no question about it. Atheists can certainly understand and even appreciate the Constitution—even though it was, by and large, a creation of men of great faith.

Personally, I know many atheists who have a much deeper understanding and appreciation of—even a reverence for—the Constitution than do the so-called Southern Baptists who currently occupy the top two positions in the executive branch of the U.S. government.

But here's where it gets really interesting. What is Gore talking about with regard to this "true spirit of tolerance"? That seems to be something of a litmus test for the presidency with Gore. What does this have to do with the price of bananas in Brazil?

Then he goes on to tell us, "I think that is incumbent upon anyone who affirms a respect for tolerance."

How much? What did he say? What's incumbent on whom? Where's he going? Hello?

The question of atheism in the White House, of course, is more than academic. Given the inappropriate accumulation of power in the U.S. presidency in recent years, the real issue is whether a man or woman who does not believe in ultimate accountability, absolute values, and divine judgment can be trusted with such an office.

The answer, of course, is no—unequivocally, undeniably, and categorically, no.

Despite their public remonstrations to the contrary, I believe the fundamental root problems with so many politicians—including some recent inhabitants of the White House—is their lack of real faith in God, their inability to subjugate their own egos and carnal urges, and their unwillingness to humble themselves as the kind of servant-leader this country knew as its first president.

Remembering the quote from chapter 9, here's how he, George

Washington, might have answered that question about an atheist in the White House:

> Of all the dispositions and habits which lead to political prosperity, Religion and morality are indispensable supports. In vain would that man claim the tribute of Patriotism, who should labor to subvert these great Pillars of human happiness, these firmest props of the duties of Men and citizens. The mere Politician, equally with the pious man ought to respect and to cherish them. A volume could not trace all their connections with private and public felicity. Let it simply be asked where is the security for property, for reputation, for life, if the sense of religious obligation desert the oaths, which are the instruments of investigation in Courts of Justice? And let us with caution indulge the supposition, that morality can be maintained without religion. Whatever may be conceded to the influence of refined education on minds of peculiar structure, reason and experience both forbid us to expect the National morality can prevail in exclusion of religious principle.
>
> 'Tis substantially true, that virtue or morality is a necessary spring of popular government. The rule indeed extends with more or less force to every species of free Government. Who that is a sincere friend to it, can look with indifference upon attempts to shake the foundation of the fabric?

Do you think one of ten contemporary politicians would even be capable of understanding Washington's statement? I doubt it.

That's a problem. Too many Americans are morally illiterate—including far too many of its purported leaders.

Washington may not have been the intellectual giant among his peers in 1776. But he was a moral giant. And he was recognized as such by all of his contemporaries. He was a truly righteous and virtuous man.

Here's what he said about self-government in his first inaugural address:

The foundations of our national policy will be laid in the pure and immutable principles of private morality, and the preeminence of free government be exemplified by all the attributes which can win the affections of its citizens, and command the respect of the world. I dwell on this prospect with every satisfaction which an ardent love for my country can inspire: since there is no truth more thoroughly established, than that there exists in the economy and course of nature, an indissoluble union between virtue and happiness; between duty and advantage; between the genuine maxims of an honest and magnanimous policy, and the solid rewards of public prosperity and felicity: since we ought to be no less persuaded that the propitious smiles of Heaven can never be expected on a nation that disregards the external rules of order and right, which Heaven itself has ordained: and since the preservation of the sacred fire of liberty, and the destiny of the republican model of government, are justly considered as deeply, perhaps as finally, staked on the experiment entrusted to the hands of the American People.

Washington cautioned his countrymen not to look for public virtue in places and people without private morality. And he warned that the great American experiment in freedom would not last without a people chastened by religious and moral principles. Indeed, as he said, the very foundation of our nation must be laid in private morality. In his farewell address, Washington returned to this theme, adding that a nation could not be happy and prosperous without being virtuous.

"Can it be, that Providence has not connected the permanent felicity of a Nation with its virtue?" he asked. "The experiment, at least, is recommended by every sentiment which enables human Nature. Alas! Is it rendered impossible by its vices?"

What did all this mean in the real world? Washington was very specific—and very practical. Even as an adolescent he drafted 110 rules of civil behavior, borrowing liberally from a text used by generations of Jesuit tutors. He carried this document on his person throughout his entire extraordinary life. These were the principles (later published as *George Washington's Rules of Civility and Decent Behavior in*

Company and Conversation) that guided him through war and peace, through trial and triumph.

More than ever two hundred years later, let us reflect on some highlights of these simple, yet profound, precepts:

1. Every action done in company ought to be with some sign of respect to those that are present.

2. When in company, put not your hands to any part of the body not usually discovered.

7. Put not off your clothes in the presence of others, nor go out your chamber half dressed.

20. The gestures of the body must be suited to the discourse you are upon.

56. Associate yourself with men of good quality if you esteem your own reputation; for 'tis better to be alone than in bad company.

58. Let your conversation be without malice or envy, for 'tis a sign of a tractable and commendable nature, and in all causes of passion permit reason to govern.

59. Never express anything unbecoming, nor act against the rules before your inferiors.

82. Undertake not what you cannot perform but be careful to keep your promise.

108. When you speak of God or his Attributes, let it be seriously . . .

109. Let your recreations be manful, not sinful.

110. Labor to keep alive in your breast that little spark of celestial fire called conscience.

Don't you wish your politicians carried around rules of behavior like these? Don't you wish your neighbors did? Don't you want your children to live up to these standards? Do you think they will learn them in government schools? Do you think we as a nation have any chance for freedom and individual liberty without embracing such precepts?

As Washington warned, "the foundation of the fabric" has indeed been "shaken." It's threadbare. And that's why I felt an urgency to call America home—to rally the faithful to take America back.

Like everything else, it starts with the Word. The Bible tells us the entire universe began with a word. People need to be engaged. They need to be focused. They need a blueprint—a road map—to find their way out of the morass.

Some people think I sound like a walking anachronism talking about God and the Bible. I get this question, or a variation on it, all the time: "Farah, what if you're wrong about God? What if there is no God? Then your Bible is a sham, and your worldview is based on a myth. So where do you get off pushing your morality on the rest of us?"

My answer is simple: First of all, I don't believe there's a snowball's chance in July that I'm wrong. No matter how you slice it, the Bible is a supernatural book—the greatest, most accurate history of mankind ever written, with more wisdom on an average page than can be found in entire modern libraries.

Accident? I don't think so. Inspired? You bet.

But let's just take the bait for a minute. Suppose I am wrong. Suppose there is no afterlife—no heaven, no hell, just here and now.

Then without a doubt the blueprint for life—whether you're talking about conducting your personal affairs or the way communities and nations interact—described in the Scriptures still leads to the most fulfilling and productive way for us to spend our time on earth.

Think about it. Can you imagine if more people lived their lives according to the rules of the Bible?

"Do unto others as you would have them do unto you."

Is there anyone out there who would like to argue with the Golden Rule? Is there anyone out there who would like to show me a greater and/or simpler commandment from any other holy book?

The first four of the Ten Commandments instruct us in the ways we are to acknowledge and worship God. But the last six tell us how to live with one another here on earth.

"Honour thy father and thy mother: that thy days may be long upon the land which the LORD thy God giveth thee" (Ex. 20:12).

Is this arguable? Is there some atheist or pagan who would challenge this commandment? Does anyone suggest that humanity would be better off if we did not honor our parents?

"Thou shalt not kill" (v. 13).

You have to admit, this is a pretty good starting point for the law. When we pass laws against murder, however, we are legislating our morality—just as surely as when we pass laws against homosexual marriage or abortion-on-demand.

"Thou shalt not commit adultery" (v. 14).

Nothing tears up marriages as completely or as often as cheating. And broken marriages are the cause of more societal problems than we can count.

"Thou shalt not steal" (v. 15).

Nobody likes it when they are the victims of theft, whether the perpetrator is a common criminal or an uncommon one—like government.

"Thou shalt not bear false witness against thy neighbour" (v. 16).

No lying. No gossiping. No falsely accusing. Good idea? I think so.

"Thou shalt not covet thy neighbour's house, thou shalt not covet thy neighbour's wife, nor his manservant, nor his maidservant, nor his ox, nor his ass, nor any thing that is thy neighbour's" (v. 17).

In other words, be thankful for what you have. Don't make designs on the property of others. Don't lie awake at night dreaming about the material things you don't have. So much evil results from jealousy.

The fact of the matter is that these basic, simple, straightforward commandments formed the basis of Western civilization—our rules, our morality, our Constitution, our laws. They served us pretty well for a long time. And the farther we drift from these basics, the more trouble people create for themselves.

The Bible provides for us the basis for self-government and a life of fulfillment. Live by the rules and you will likely live longer and more happily than someone who doesn't. Any doubts about that?

So what if I am wrong? Will my faith leave us worse off or better off? I think the answer is clear and obvious.

Now, the question might be even more enlightening when redirected to those who ask it. What if we scrapped the old rules? What if we decided the Bible was nothing but an old book written by uptight, dead white guys? Suppose we rewrote the Book of Life according to the conventions of modernism, humanism, or secularism?

What would be the ground rules of such a society? If it feels good, do it? Do unto others before they do unto you? And what would be the moral authority for this other code? If there is no ultimate, Supreme Being to judge our actions, then who is to make the rules? Government? Who is to endow us with our human rights? The United Nations?

You know the answer to these questions, my friends. Just search your soul for them. God has etched His moral code on the hearts of every person. You may not believe in God, but, nevertheless, He believes in you.

If I'm wrong, I will have lived a sometimes difficult, yet rewarding and fulfilling life of expectation, hope, and joy. I will not have missed out on anything meaningful. If I'm right, I get to spend eternity in paradise.

But what if you're wrong? What kind of a world would you have built? How much real happiness will you have experienced? And when your life is over, what will you have missed?

Without morality, self-government is doomed. That's a fact. It's also a fact that people need information.

It was James Madison in *Notes on Virginia* who said, "A popular government without popular information, or the means of acquiring it, is but a prologue to a farce or a tragedy, or perhaps both. Knowledge will forever govern ignorance, and a people who mean to be their own governors must arm themselves with the power which knowledge gives."

We live in an "information age," they tell us. Therefore, we must be smarter and wiser than any generation heretofore, right?

Wrong. In fact, all one really need do is read the above quote or one of hundreds of other similar gems from our founders to understand how little we know and understand today. It's this fact that prompted me to launch WorldNetDaily.com. It's this fact that prompted Elizabeth and me to homeschool our kids. We not only need a basic sense of morality, but we also need some wisdom. We need to know what's really going on in our world.

It is impossible for people to govern themselves without a basic sense of morality—of right and wrong. Without conscience, the only deterrent to antisocial behavior is punishment. While punishment is a secondary necessity in even the most moral societies, by itself it can never adequately discourage bad behavior.

Secondarily, a self-governing people must be informed. They must understand their surroundings. They must comprehend how the world works. They must be able to discern truth from fiction. They must have a mechanism for seeking knowledge. They must be equipped with the tools to recognize it when they see it.

Do I have to point out that America is losing its ability for self-government in both of these areas?

Despite the fact that more information is more readily available—faster, cheaper, and easier than ever before in history—Americans are, in many ways, less informed, less educated, less moral, and less wise than any previous generation.

This is the central crisis we face as a nation. It will destroy us unless we change direction.

Americans don't perceive the threat. They believe falsely that people only lose their freedom in violent and sudden usurpations—by being conquered by outside enemies or through political revolutions and coups. They believe it can't happen here. They take for granted that what we have here in America has always been and will always be.

Madison could set them straight on that score too.

"I believe there are more instances of the abridgment of the freedom of the people by gradual and silent encroachments of those in power than by violent and sudden usurpations," he said.

And that's the way it is happening in America. The frog is slowly simmering in the pot. Before he realizes the heat is about to kill him, it will be too late to jump.

The good news is that there's a remnant of Americans who understand what's happening today and who are going to fight for freedom again. I'm very hopeful that, with God's help, we can establish freedom and liberty again in America just as our founders did in the eighteenth century.

I'm very upbeat that we can restore freedom in America. I think the founders showed the way. We should emulate their example. I think we have a chance to overthrow the new empire peacefully.

But Americans have to learn to say no. They have to say no to the government indoctrination centers we call public schools. They have to say no to taxes by minimizing by every legal means what they pay in tribute to Washington. They have to fight back by taking control of government locally and declaring sovereignty from Washington. They have to resist participation in election charades where there is no choice— where no candidate truly supports the Constitution in word and deed.

Are you with me? If so, maybe together we can rediscover freedom and independence once again. We can take America back.

★ 14 ★

FIGHTING BACK

In the beginning of a change the patriot is a scarce man, and brave, and hated and scorned. When his cause succeeds, the timid join him, for then it costs nothing to be a patriot.

—MARK TWAIN

IF YOU WANT TO TAKE AMERICA BACK FROM THE WASHINGTON Empire the way our forefathers claimed it from the British Empire, you've got to have courage. You've got to have faith. You've got to have strength. This fight will be no less difficult than the one waged by the colonials.

What did the U.S. founders do first when they realized the time had come to fight?

They got down on their knees and prayed fervently for God's divine intervention in their struggle. Over and over again when they faced seemingly insurmountable odds—whether it was the wrath of nature at Valley Forge or political divisions in Independence Hall—they stopped their fretting and got down on their knees.

Today we're told by those who see government as the final authority in the lives of men that our founders were a bunch of deists—people who didn't really believe God intervened in human affairs.

Benjamin Franklin, they say, is a perfect example. Yet, read Franklin's stirring words, spoken in the federal framing convention in 1787, when consensus seemed hopeless. He called the convention to prayer with the following words: "I have lived, Sir, a long time, and the longer I live, the more convincing proofs I see of this truth—that God governs in the affairs of men. And if a sparrow cannot fall to the ground without His notice, is it probable that an empire can rise without His aid? . . . I also believe that without His concurring aid we shall succeed in this political building no better than the Builders of Babel."

Does that sound like a man who believes God no longer intervenes in the affairs of men?

We need to follow the example of such men. We need to call together believers for prayer for our nation. For all of you who agree with me that our nation is adrift—heading off perilously in the wrong direction—we need to humble ourselves and seek God's help.

This is Step 1 in taking America back: Repent and pray.

Historians often say that the first War of Independence was inspired in the pulpits of colonial America. I know there are many Christian leaders and pastors who are reading this book and wondering what their role is in returning America to freedom and morality. I have news for you: Your role is the central role. You need to use your positions of moral authority and moral clarity as Jonathan Mayhew, Samuel West, and John Witherspoon did.

Today, too many Christians are timid. Many justify their timidity on the basis of Scriptures, which, these folks apparently believe, mean Christians should not resist evil perpetrated by government. The first reference is found in Matthew 22:21, where Jesus said, "Render therefore unto Caesar the things which are Caesar's; and unto God the things that are God's" (see also Mark 12:17 and Luke 20:25).

The second Scripture cited by readers is found in Romans 13, in which the apostle Paul advocates submission to earthly rulers (vv. 1–7). A great many contemporary American Christians—including many pastors—have come to believe the central duty of good citizens and churches is to "render unto Caesar."

I strongly suggest that my dear misguided Christian friends spend a little time reading the great debates that precipitated the War for Independence—all of which took place among men far more learned in the Scriptures than the average contemporary Christian.

"Unlimited submission and obedience is due to none but God alone," said Samuel West in 1776. "He alone has an uncontrollable sovereignty over us, because He alone is unchangeable good. He never will nor can require of us, consistent with His nature and attributes, anything which is not fit and reasonable. His commands are all just and good. And to suppose that He has given to any particular set of men a power to require obedience to that which is unreasonable, cruel, and unjust, is robbing the Deity of His justice and goodness."

It's important to consider the circumstances and the audience behind Jesus' instructions to "render unto Caesar." The Sadducees were attempting to trap Jesus into advocating open contempt for Caesar. He recognized their wicked and hypocritical little game and answered them with a totally truthful response that astonished everyone.

But think about it. There are two components to Jesus' words. We are to "render therefore unto Caesar the things which are Caesar's," but we are also to "render . . . unto God the things that are God's." Well, everything ultimately belongs to God. But, most of all, this injunction by Jesus instructs us that government laws cannot trump God's laws—ever.

If government commands you to do evil, as a Christian you must resist. There is no alternative. Citing the "render unto Caesar" line is an excuse not to be accountable to God—nothing more, nothing less. Furthermore, it needs to be pointed out that in America we don't have a caesar. Never have, never will. You see, our system of government is called a free republic and it is based on the concept of constitutional self-government. We have no "rulers" in America—except ourselves and our God. We believe in the rule of law, not the rule of men.

This is an important distinction, not a semantic one.

Nowhere in the Bible does it teach us to obey evil rulers. Nowhere. Quite the contrary. In fact, the Bible has inspired more nonviolent civil disobedience movements than any other religious document. The example of Jesus and the apostles was to submit to arrest, submit to being jailed, even submit to execution. But in no way can one derive from biblical example that we are to do evil because we are told to do so by government.

I for one am not accountable to any caesar, thank God. I am accountable to my Creator. My rights and responsibilities as a free man descend not from government, but from God Almighty.

The greatest acts of moral courage in the last two thousand years have been the countless examples of individuals standing up to tyrants against all odds. Sadly, it seems many modern American Christians are content to sit on their duffs and condone evil because of their own scriptural illiteracy and moral blindness.

But all that is almost beside the point. American Christians could in all likelihood take America back peacefully—without lifting a hand, without firing a shot. They have the numbers. What they lack is the leadership. It's time for the pastors of this country to begin acting like the heroic pastors of the colonial era.

What do Christians need to do to take America back? It all starts when we learn to say "No." Americans need to learn to resist. They've got to change from a spirit of compliance to government to a spirit of obedience to God.

What does this mean in the political arena? For starters, moral people—citizens who consider themselves accountable to God first and who uphold the Constitution as the law of the land in America—must oppose any and all politicians who won't strictly adhere to that law. There can be no ifs, ands, or buts about this. You can't vote for the lesser of two evils because that is still voting for evil. It's better not to participate in evil at all.

This is a hard one for many Americans who have become conditioned to the idea that voting is their central civic duty. It may be—

but not if it means supporting evil, even a shade of evil. I've been called irresponsible for making this statement. Many Americans have become convinced they have a sacred duty to vote—even if it means pulling the lever for an unqualified, hyperambitious dolt who wouldn't know the Constitution if he wiped his feet on it.

So many Americans say that failure to vote for one of the two major party candidates in any election is tantamount to "throwing your vote away." I say voting for an illegitimate candidate—one who will not live under the rule of law and abide by the Constitution—is throwing your vote away.

If you don't have a choice, don't vote. Don't pretend you have a choice. Don't dignify a corrupt system with your participation in a charade.

Do you want to understand what's wrong with the false paradigm offered by our current political system? Do you want to know how our kids are being programmed to rely on government as a parent and as their god? Do you want to see how we are losing our freedoms in America?

The answers hit me like a ton of bricks one day a couple of years ago when my family was touring the historic sites in Philadelphia. After visiting the Liberty Bell and touring Independence Hall, we stopped in a nearby gift shop. Inside, a survey was being distributed by a group called the Philadelphia Citizens for Children and Youth.

It was titled "If I were elected president of the United States, I would . . ." Are you ready to take the questionnaire? You get to choose three answers. Here goes:

a. improve the schools

b. make sure the air and water are clean

c. protect kids in their homes and in their neighborhoods

d. make sure there are lots of after-school programs

e. make sure that homeless people are taken care of

f. make sure everyone has enough to eat

g. make sure that all kids live in safe and sturdy homes

h. see that there is peace on earth

i. make sure that there are lots of parks and other places where kids can be in and learn about nature

j. help parents learn how to care for their kids

What was the point of this survey? Obviously to condition kids to believe government—and especially the executive branch of the federal government—has the power and the duty to intervene in the lives of individual citizens at every level in every conceivable way.

I can think of no more dangerous idea we could teach our kids. And the fact that this is happening in Independence Hall—the most historic site in America commemorating our nation's fight for individual freedom, national sovereignty, and self-governance—simply adds insult to injury.

Even more dangerous is the fact that both parties in Washington buy into the concept—in action if not in rhetoric—that the fundamental answers to our societal problems can be found in deeper federal involvement in schools and increased spending on programs that could never work even if they were constitutional.

The presidency was never designed for such powers. The federal government was never meant to be involved in every facet of our lives. That's the urgent lesson we should be teaching our kids. We should be teaching them self-reliance, personal responsibility, and vigilance against tyranny.

The only things elected officials in Washington could do to solve the problems named on the survey would be to disengage from them—to admit that central control is a mistake, one forbidden by our Constitution.

What I would do if I were elected president:

Improve the schools? Sure, by working tirelessly to end all federal involvement in education. Period. The only way to improve schools is by making decisions at the local level—meaning the family.

Clean up air and water? Sure, by selling off the millions of acres of federal land accumulated by the government over the last two hundred years and by restoring the concept of private property rights to individuals. The fact is that people are generally much better stewards of their own property than government is.

Protect kids in their homes? Sure. I would push Congress to build a strategic nuclear defense to make sure that Chinese, North Korean, Iranian, and Russian missiles never land on them. I would promote real civil defense to minimize death and destruction planned by terrorists at war with us now and those that will be planned by future enemies.

After-school programs? Yes, I'd push Congress to eliminate the income tax so mothers could afford to return to the home and provide the best kind of after-school programs for their kids—loving home care.

Take care of the homeless? Yes, I'd use the presidency as a bully pulpit to remind the churches that this is their responsibility—not government's.

Make sure everyone has enough to eat? For starters, I'd try to kill all the agricultural subsidies that encourage farmers not to grow food. Then I would fight for the elimination of the death tax so family farms could remain family farms.

Safe and sturdy homes? Yes, I would condemn all those federal government projects that are little more than death traps and prisons for people seduced into dependency by Washington.

Peace on earth? Something I would pray for night and day—and encourage other Americans to do the same. But my job as president would be to work tirelessly to protect the people of the United States. Peace through strength has served us well when we have applied the principle.

Parks and nature? Has anyone ever noticed that the most restricted parkland in the country is controlled by the federal government? Indeed, something needs to be done about that. Let the kids and their parents have access to their land.

Help parents learn how to care for their kids? Hmm. Somehow I just don't think there's a role for the president—except perhaps to tell them they've been lied to for too many years. The government is a fearsome nanny.

In other words, I would promote self-reliance, personal responsibility, and self-government, and I would focus the government on the few, specific, limited powers to which it is authorized under the Constitution. Period. End of story.

Am I running for president? No. This is not the way to change this country. This is not the way to take America back. The way to begin doing that is in our own families, in our own churches, in our own communities, and in our own counties and states. What do I mean?

For example, let's reconsider the schools. Here's a radical idea for parents and students in government schools: *Drop out!*

That's right. I know this idea goes against the grain of what you're being told by establishment politicians of the left and the right. I know it will make the National Education Association very angry. I know I will be called irresponsible for giving this advice. I don't care. Been there, done that.

The simple truth is clear. Government-run schools are not educating our kids. At best they serve as day-care centers. At their worst, they are the moral equivalent of prisons and political indoctrination camps.

Why are kids killing each other in school today? C. Bradley Thompson, an associate professor of history and politics at Ashland University, says that's what happens when you confine people like laboratory animals and conduct the equivalent of behavioral vivisection on them.

"The explanation for all these shootings might very well be found in the destruction of the minds and souls of America's young people by an education establishment bent on using our children as guinea pigs for their bizarre experiments in schooling," he explains in a *Bangkok Post* op-ed. "The fact of the matter is that most U.S. public schools today are intellectual and moral wastelands."

Thompson relates a familiar theme heard from others who teach recent high-school graduates:

- Students don't believe in much and are unwilling to make moral judgments.

- Students are taught to have artificially inflated opinions of themselves and are unwilling to tolerate criticism.

- They are poorly educated.

- They hate their high-school experience.

"The result is an explosive mixture of nihilism, narcissism, ignorance and resentment," Thompson writes.

The solution is not more testing, more spending on schools, more centralization of authority, requiring students to spend more time in schools, nor repeating the mistakes of the past.

It's time to begin pulling the plug on government education—beginning with Washington's role. But that won't happen if you wait for politicians in Washington to wise up. There's no way that will ever happen from the top down. Privatizing education, reinvigorating it with the proper rewards and incentives, is a long-term process.

If you want to save your kids, you need an alternative now. Almost any alternative is better than warehousing your children in government facilities and abdicating your authority over them to the state.

Encourage your kids—especially those in high school—to just drop out. I know this sounds crazy to many of you out there. I know you don't hear this from any other quarter. But until parents and students just start saying no, there's no hope of extricating America from state control of every aspect of our lives.

What's the alternative to the government indoctrination centers? You might be able to find a good private school in your area. But be warned: Many of them have become mired in the politically correct claptrap of the NEA and the government-education blob. The starting point for change is dropping out—then searching for the right alternative.

As I've already detailed, I believe homeschooling is the best route. Many parents are afraid of it. They don't feel equipped to teach their own kids. Believe me, you can do no worse than the government—and in the process you will be saving your kids' minds and souls.

You can do better for your children. You have an obligation to do better for your children. Education is your responsibility, not the state's. Don't wait for vouchers. Don't wait for the president to save you. Don't wait for Congress. Don't waste your time trying to work within the system. Don't even waste your time with the PTA meetings, nor getting involved in ways to improve your local government school system. The system is corrupt from top to bottom, and you will only end up frustrated, burned out, delaying the inevitable, and propping up a thoroughly corrupt and evil system.

Start with your children. Make them examples of what parents can achieve without government intervention and meddling.

You can start by teaching them right from wrong—something they will never learn in government lockup.

Right now millions of Americans have already made this decision in recent years and it is paying off for them personally and for their children. Those kids are scoring higher on tests. They are winning awards. They are happier. They are achieving great things. They are *educated*.

Why is this so important to restoring freedom in America? Why is this such a key element of the battle plan? Because, as the founders understood, only an educated people can govern themselves.

"I know of no safe depository of the ultimate powers of the society but the people themselves," wrote Thomas Jefferson. "And if we think them not enlightened enough to exercise their control with a wholesome discretion, the remedy is not to take it from them, but to inform their discretion by education."

It should be incentive enough for millions more to join the millions who have already left the government school system to know that this is the best solution—the only solution—for their children.

But there's another reason we should pull our kids out of the system: I can't think of any other single form of peaceful rebellion that will bring about more rapidly the crumbling of the statist infrastructure. This is the first shot in the war to take America back. We must first take our children back—reclaim them as our own, reclaim them in the name of God, reclaim them from the corrupt halls of secular humanism.

Not only will this have a dramatic and positive impact on our kids, but it will be the first death blow to the overreaching government. Nonparticipation is a powerful weapon. How long do you think Americans will tolerate coercive taxation to support other people's schools? Not very long. The whole system will begin to collapse of its own dead weight—just like the Soviet Empire crashed before our eyes.

This is how we should fight the Second American Revolution. We must declare our independence from the throes of unconstitutional, illegal, and illegitimate government first—just as our founders did. The first step, today, is getting our kids out of their clutches. Radical? Maybe so. But more and more smart and responsible people are with me on this—from Dr. James Dobson to Dr. Laura Schlessinger, both of whom have called for the public-school exodus on their widely syndicated radio shows.

Are you ready to do this—for your own children's good and the good of the country?

Again, this is radical. This is resistance. This is the first stage of righteous rebellion. And if more Americans followed this simple prescription, the statist system would fall like a house of cards.

There's another important step: Don't waste your energies campaigning for a presidential candidate. Instead, focus your energy where it will count—at the local level. Taking America back begins by taking back your city councils, your county boards, your zoning boards, your sheriff's departments—all the local government bodies. Then use those agencies and governing bodies to resist Washington's power grab, to say no to federal intrusion, to fight Big Government's mandates.

This is already happening in several areas of the country with great results. The federal government knows its limitations. It has no lawful power outside of its limited jurisdiction. The only way it can impose its will on local communities and in the various states is through force of arms.

What if it comes to that? What if there is that kind of repression? What if Washington refuses to yield power it has usurped from the states and from sovereign, self-governing individuals like you and me? What if the government uses its awesome power against its own citizens?

Then, my friends, it's time to do what was attempted back in 1861 and what others—including columnist Walter Williams—are already suggesting today. It's time to reconsider the idea of secession.

When I first began writing about the need for a Second American Revolution or a Second War of Independence, many Southerners corrected me. They explained that that conflict, otherwise known as the War Between the States, had already been fought and lost. They have a point. Indeed, the motivations of many in the Confederacy were quite pure in that regard—a desire to live up to the promises of the U.S. Constitution, to test the principle of a voluntary union, to promote self-government and the rights of the states.

But we don't want to refight the War Between the States—the bloodiest conflict ever for Americans.

The battle to take America back won't be a regional contest. It won't be clouded by the issue of slavery. But it may someday involve breaking the bands that tie us together so that those of us who still believe in the concept of self-government might be free to test it.

I know it's radical. I know it's not a topic being discussed on the Sunday-morning talk shows. I know it's not a subject of op-eds in the *New York Times*. But the more I think about it, the more I agree it may be the only political solution that makes sense for an America that has lost its sense of mission and the original intent of those who wrote the Declaration of Independence and the Constitution.

"If one group of people prefers government control and management of people's lives, and another prefers liberty and a desire to be left alone, should they be required to fight, antagonize one another, and risk bloodshed and loss of life in order to impose their preferences, or should they be able to peaceably part company and go their separate ways?" Williams once asked in his Creators Syndicate column.

I say it's time to part company. So does Williams. And so do a growing number of other observers and political thinkers who see little chance to turn our government around through the normal political machinery.

"Like a marriage that has gone bad, I believe there are enough irreconcilable differences between those who want to control and those who want to be left alone that divorce is the only peaceable alternative," Williams writes. "Just as in a marriage, where vows are broken, our human rights protections guaranteed by the U.S. Constitution have been grossly violated by a government instituted to protect them. Americans who are responsible for and support constitutional abrogation have no intention of mending their ways."

As we listen to politicians and parties debate which one has the better programs to deepen the federal government's illegitimate role in education, health, and dozens of other aspects of American life, it's clear that those who cherish liberty and the Constitution have no choice in most elections anymore.

Article 1, Section 8, of the Constitution clearly enumerates the activities for which Congress is authorized to tax and spend. If there is any doubt about what those words mean, read the words of the man who wrote the Constitution, James Madison, in Federalist 45:

> The powers delegated by the proposed Constitution to the federal government are few and defined. Those which are to remain in the state governments are numerous and indefinite. The former will be exercised principally on external objects, as war, peace, negotiation and foreign commerce . . . The powers reserved to the several states will extend to all the objects which in the ordinary course of affairs, concern the lives and liberties and properties of the people, and the internal order, improvement and prosperity of the state.

Seems clear to me. So where's the argument?

Nowhere in the enumerated powers of Congress is there authority to tax and spend for Social Security, government schools, farm subsidies, bank bailouts, food stamps, creating official "art," disaster relief, national police forces, and other activities that represent roughly two-thirds of the federal budget.

"Neither is there authority for Congress' mandates to the states and people about how they may use their land, the speed at which they can drive, whether a library has wheelchair ramps and the gallons of water used per toilet flush," writes Williams. "A list of congressional violations of the letter and spirit of the Constitution is virtually without end."

As Williams and others see it, Americans who wish to live free have two options: "We can resist, fight and risk bloodshed to force America's tyrants to respect our liberties and human rights, or we can seek a peaceful resolution of our irreconcilable differences by separating. That can be done by people in several states, say Texas and Louisiana, controlling their legislatures and then issuing a unilateral declaration of independence just as the founders did in 1776."

Can such a result be achieved through the ballot box? No, Williams says. And, more important, he adds, "Liberty shouldn't require a vote. It's a God-given or natural right."

It's time to move this debate forward—front and center. It's time to begin asking the real questions. It's time to restore liberty to America—whatever it takes. It's time to take America back.

It's time to restore "power to the people."

I bet you haven't heard that phrase in a while. It was widely misused and abused thirty to thirty-five years ago by some whose desire to shift power really had nothing to do with serving the interests of the people.

But it was a good phrase—one that was easy to support and understand. It was co-opted by a movement whose ultimate objective, whether all the participants knew it or not, was to centralize power, to take it away from the people, to serve the interests of the state.

Maybe it's time to resurrect that phrase. After all, there are many forces today trying desperately to centralize authority—nationally, globally, corporately. Yet, technology is giving us opportunities to make those forces irrelevant—if only we recognize the chance we have.

THE TAKING AMERICA BACK
12-STEP ACTION PROGRAM

1. Get down on your knees in prayer; America needs spiritual revival and renewal.

2. Stop voting for the lesser of two evils—never vote for any candidate who doesn't support 100 percent the Constitution of the United States.

3. Pull your children out of government schools now! Teach your children right from wrong and provide them a sound education—preferably in your own home.

4. Find good reliable sources of news—like WorldNetDaily.com—and be informed.

5. Insulate your children from the effects of the popular culture—and don't let it seduce you, either.

6. Arm yourself and your family.

7. Take control of your own community—city councils, zoning boards, county boards.

8. Use your local power to resist federal intrusion and mandates.

9. Fight the tax man with all your might, skill, and determination.

10. Always teach and practice freedom, self-reliance, and personal responsibility.

11. Distribute copies of this book to all your friends and relatives—and to your priest, rabbi, or minister.

12. Network with other like-minded people across the nation through the Taking America Back Web site (takingamericaback.com).

<h1>★ 15 ★</h1>

<h1>IS THERE HOPE?</h1>

For unto us a child is born, unto us a son is given: and the government shall be upon his shoulder: and his name shall be called Wonderful, Counsellor, The mighty God, The everlasting Father, The Prince of Peace. Of the increase of his government and peace there shall be no end, upon the throne of David, and upon his kingdom, to order it, and to establish it with judgment and with justice from henceforth even for ever. The zeal of the LORD of hosts will perform this.

—ISAIAH 9:6–7

Never give up, never give in, never, never, never, never—in nothing, great or small, large or petty—never give in except to convictions of honor and good sense.

—WINSTON CHURCHILL

YES, AMERICA, THERE IS HOPE. YOU CAN TAKE AMERICA back. But the battle will not be an easy one.

The question is: How badly do you want it?

Are you willing to sacrifice as Washington, Jefferson, Madison, and others did in establishing it? Are you willing to do more than complain? Are you willing to take action?

Are you willing to ensure that your motives are pure?

Motives? What do motives have to do with reestablishing freedom in America?

Back in the 1960s there was a movement, spawned in America, that sought to overthrow the status quo—to fight "the establishment," to create a new paradigm, to end war, to seek "justice" and "equality."

The fruits of that movement were more death, destruction, ruined families, and a breakdown in morality. Why? Because the seeds of that "revolution" were bad from the beginning.

Man has always been tempted by rebellion. It's in his nature. It's in his blood.

Remember when Pontius Pilate held Jesus of Nazareth captive? He knew Jesus was innocent.

"I find no fault in this man," Pilate said.

He held another prisoner—a man named Barabbas. Barabbas is an enigmatic character. We don't know a great deal about him from Scripture. But he is described in Matthew 27:16 as "a notable prisoner"—that is to say "notorious." In Mark 15:7, it is said he "made insurrection" and "committed murder in the insurrection." In Luke 23:19 he is described as being guilty of sedition and murder. In John 18:40 he is described as a "robber."

It is thought that Barabbas may have been a leader of a group attempting to free Israel of Roman rule—a seemingly worthy goal. But what were his motives?

We may get a clue from his name. In Aramaic, Barabbas literally means "son of his father." We might assume that Barabbas was attempting, through rebellion—through force of arms—to reestablish the throne of his Hebrew father, "King David," and the patriarchs Abraham, Isaac, and Jacob.

Barabbas's father was a real man, a mortal, a fleshly human being. Jesus, on the other hand, is the Son of His Father in heaven.

Pilate gave the people a choice that day—they could free Jesus, the Son of His Father in heaven, or Barabbas, the son of an earthly man. We all know the crowd chose Barabbas.

If and when we choose to fight for our freedom in America, again, we must be careful about our motives. Are we seeking to establish a righteous nation under God or are we merely fighting to do "our patriotic duty"?

Think about it. The word *patriot* is derived from the word for "father" or "fatherland."

Misguided "patriotism" is not a pure motive. We must fight for a higher cause. And if we fight, we must fight with the weapons of our Father in heaven, not the carnal weapons of man.

In the '60s, some fought a "revolution for the hell of it." In the 21st century, if we are to succeed, if we are to win a meaningful victory and if we are to be justified in our fight, we need to fight a "revolution for the heaven of it."

Washington, Jefferson, Madison et al., understood the necessity of pure motives and the need for calling on all the powers of heaven to intercede on their behalf. While they fought the yoke of oppression by a foreign power in America, the French, too, fought a revolution without spiritual purpose, without studying the Scriptures, without pure motives. The result was more bloodshed, more oppression, less freedom.

We do have a great hope in heaven. For those of us who understand the Scriptures, we know the real battle has already been fought and won. This life on earth is short. If we put our faith in Jesus Christ, our eternal rewards are set. Therefore, our number one job here on earth is to spread the good news. In doing so, we can only make our time on earth more worth living.

Yet as the founding fathers of this nation showed, when government becomes a stumbling block to that goal—when it denies God, when it places itself above God, when it serves another god—that government is no longer legitimate. It no longer binds free men and women who serve the One True God.

Yes, America, there is hope—if we call on God and keep our eyes upon Him. If we get our direction from Him, we literally cannot lose. There is not a doubt in my mind that this is our sacred duty, just as it was the sacred duty of Washington, Jefferson, and Madison to throw off the yoke of oppression in 1776.

But it will not be easy. Have no illusions about that. It always requires courage to stand up and fight—no matter what form that fight takes.

"It is natural to man to indulge in the illusions of hope," said Patrick Henry. "We are apt to shut our eyes against a painful truth . . . Is this the part of wise men, engaged in a great and arduous struggle for liberty? Are we disposed to be of the number of those who, having eyes, see not, and having ears, hear not, the things which so clearly concern their temporal salvation? For my part, whatever anguish of spirit it may cost, I am willing to know the whole truth; to know the worst and to provide for it."

Miracles do happen. They happened in the early days of America's struggle for freedom, and they can and will happen again in the fight to take America back—if Americans will repent of their sins, get down on their knees in submission to God, and cry out to Him for help.

Many Americans—especially in the postwar Baby Boom generation—tend to think change comes slowly. They look around them and believe, incorrectly, that things have always been this way. They take for granted the blessings of their lives and believe they are powerless to address the curses.

It's not true. Change in this world is constant. Change often happens quickly—both positive changes and negative changes can occur practically overnight. You may look around, like me, and see Americans losing touch with the great promises of their independence. It's easy to become disillusioned, pessimistic—to throw up your hands and say, "What's the use?"

I believe freedom can break out across America and around the world as quickly as an epidemic can spread. Perhaps this book will provide what best-selling author Malcolm Gladwell dubbed *The Tipping Point*. Little things make a big difference in the world. Change doesn't always come gradually, Gladwell explains, but often all in one dramatic moment. Ideas and trends often spread nearly inexplicably as quickly as a contagious illness.

There's no question the world's institutions are breaking down. The schools. Law enforcement. Government itself. The rule of law.

This is no accident. Long before the political institutions we rely on to maintain civil order began to crumble, our major cultural institutions lost their moorings. The entertainment industry. The press. Academia. Even the churches.

We're on the downward end of a slippery slope. People recognize it. As we stride through this new millennium, it's only natural that people are asking, "With all the bad news in the world, is there any hope?"

What can we do? To whom can we write? Whom should we call? Is there anyone we can trust?

I believe we're nearing the tipping point—the time at which the trends we see will reverse themselves suddenly and seemingly miraculously. You can be a part of that revolution without firing a shot, without suffering through a hungry winter at Valley Forge, and without necessarily marching on Washington.

There is order in this universe. There is One greater than us on whom we can depend. He's always there for us. And He's got a plan for our personal salvation as well as a plan for a world without end.

Unlike our politicians and those who control our cultural institutions, He's always listening to us—from the innermost yearnings of our hearts to the unspoken words of our contemplative minds.

Sometimes knowledge of the world's evils can be a heavy burden. Yet we can't run away from them. We can't isolate ourselves from them. We can't pretend they don't exist.

The apostle Paul was confronted with this same dilemma. He explained that God's righteousness was revealed in the Scriptures and through the birth, life, death, and resurrection of Christ—"the righteousness of God revealed from faith to faith." (Rom. 1:17).

At times like these—trying times—Paul explained further that the righ-teous will live by faith.

I don't think I could carry on for another day without absolute faith that righteousness would someday triumph in this world. There's too much pain, too much suffering, too much sin, too much evil. Perhaps it will take the Lord's return to restore freedom and morality. Perhaps it is very near. But I don't think the Scriptures teach us to wait passively for God to take care of the world. We are taught to occupy until He comes. We are taught to be salt and light.

Indeed, I believe, our sad state of affairs today is a direct result of forgetting God. It's the result of man exercising his own wisdom rather than relying on the laws of God. The Bible is replete with horror stories of such folly—beginning in the Garden of Eden and ending on the cross.

"And it shall be, if thou do at all forget the LORD thy God, and walk after other gods, and serve them, and worship them, I testify against you this day that ye shall surely perish," we are warned in Deuteronomy 8:19.

"The wicked shall be turned into hell, and all the nations that forget God," we're told in Psalm 9:17.

For six thousand years of human history, the story has been the same. Someone, some leader, some group, some city, some nation, even the entire world decides it knows better than God. The consequences are always dire. Whenever God is removed from the equation, something bad fills the vacuum.

Have you ever noticed that? What filled the vacuum in ancient Israel when they forgot about God? Conquest and slavery. What filled the vacuum in the Soviets' lives when they forgot God? The all-knowing, all-powerful state. What's filling the vacuum in Americans' lives now that we have forgotten God?

Some people tell me I shouldn't write about spiritual matters. They say, as a journalist, I don't know what I'm talking about. They say I lose credibility on more important issues. They say I compromise my objectivity.

To them I say, there are no more important issues than this. There is no neutral ground in the spiritual warfare consuming this universe. And there is nothing I am more certain about than this: A better day is coming. Why not get ready by taking America back? Why not fulfill God's will in your own life and in the life of your country?

Is there a doubt in your mind that this is what God would have us do? Don't you think He wants us to reestablish the promises of America—the one nation under God born of a creed?

What's stopping us?

Nothing.

Now stand up and join me in taking America back.

ABOUT
THE AUTHOR

JOSEPH FARAH IS EDITOR, FOUNDER, AND CHIEF EXECUTIVE officer of WorldNetDaily.com, the Internet's largest independent news site. He is a veteran newspaper editor—having run the *Sacramento Union,* the oldest daily paper west of the Mississippi, the news department of the *Los Angeles Herald Examiner,* and other dailies and weeklies. He is the coauthor of *This Land Is Our Land* and collaborated with Rush Limbaugh on the 1993–94 No. 1 best-selling nonfiction book, *See, I Told You So.* He has also collaborated with Hal Lindsey, Greg Laurie, and others on more than a dozen books.

WorldNetDaily.com.

WorldNetDaily.com (or WND.com) is a fiercely independent news Web site committed to hard-hitting investigative reporting of government waste, fraud, and abuse.

Rated a top-1,000 Web site by Alexa.com, WND.com is a leading news Web site in both traffic and influence, attracting 3 million unique visitors a month and breaking some of the biggest, most significant and notable investigative and enterprising stories in recent years.

Founded by Joseph and Elizabeth Farah in May 1997, WND.com's editorial policy reflects the old-fashioned notion that the principal role of the free press in a free society is to serve as a watchdog on government, exposing abuse wherever and whenever it is found.

WND BOOKS

A DIVISION OF THOMAS NELSON, INC.

The pen is indeed mightier than the sword. In an age where swords are being rattled all over the world, a new voice has emerged. An unprecedented partnership between WorldNetDaily, the leading independent Internet news site, and Thomas Nelson, Inc., one of the leading publishers in America, has brought about a new book-publishing venture—WND Books.

You can find WND Books at your favorite bookstore, or by visiting the Web site www.WorldNetDaily.com.

CENTER OF THE STORM: PRACTICING PRINCIPLED LEADERSHIP IN TIMES OF CRISIS—Former Florida Secretary of State Katherine Harris discusses behind-the-scenes negotiations, backroom bartering, and the twelve essential principles that helped her not just survive but thrive during the infamous 2000 presidential election vote recount.

ISBN 0-7852-6443-4

THE SAVAGE NATION: SAVING AMERICA FROM THE LIBERAL ASSAULT ON OUR BORDERS, LANGUAGE, AND CULTURE— Michael Savage, host of the forth largest radio talk show, uses bold, biting, and hilarious straight talk to take aim at the sacred cows of our ever-eroding culture and the "group of psychopaths" known as PETA, the ACLU, and the liberal media.

ISBN 0-7852-6353-5

FIRST STRIKE—With an impressive array of facts, Jack Cashill and James Sanders show the relationship between the TWA Flight 800 disaster of July 1996 and the September 11 attacks in 2001 and proclaim how and why the American government has attempted to cover up the truth.

Available March 2003—ISBN 0-7852-6354-3

AT ANY PRICE—Patricia Roush's girls were kidnapped more than sixteen years ago and taken by their Saudi father to the kingdom of Saudi Arabia. In the midst of this tragic set of circumstances came an ongoing, demoralizing struggle with the U.S. government and the Saudi kingdom to reunite her with her children.

Available April 2003— ISBN 0-7852-6365-9